RIDIN

Christine

Illustrated by Christine Bousfield

AN ARMADA ORIGINAL

Riding For Fun was first published in
Armada in 1976 by Fontana Paperbacks
14 St James's Place, London SW1A 1PS
This impression 1979

© Christine Pullein-Thompson 1976

Printed in Great Britain by
William Collins Sons & Co. Ltd, London and Glasgow

Contents

Foreword

Having a pony should be fun – most of the time at any rate. If it's causing family rows, scenes at shows, or floods of tears, it isn't being fun – it's like school when you have endless exams. Something has made it into a toil instead of a pleasure.

You don't need to win prizes to have fun with a pony – there are so many other things you can do besides compete. There are picnic rides and hunting, running your own horse show and teaching your pony tricks; there are long distance rides with tents and maps or hours spent exploring on your own; there are treasure hunts, or pony club camp with fifty or more riders. You can shop on a pony too, if the shop-keeper doesn't mind, or visit friends.

Looking after a pony doesn't need to be dreary at all – and at least it's more fun than doing housework or washing the car – or should be.

This book is written to encourage you to enjoy your pony more. But I hope it will help *him* to enjoy *you* more as well, for ponies like fun as much as you do. They hate bad-tempered riders and going the same dreary way day after day – they like friends and new faces (pony faces of course!).

Competitions of all Kinds and How to Run Your Own Show

Gymkhanas

Riding in gymkhanas can be tremendous fun if not taken too seriously. On the other hand, if you don't take any trouble at all, being last in every event can be very depressing. Even the slowest pony can be good at something. Teach your pony to gallop from a standstill, to stop at 'Whoa!' and you are half way to winning prizes. Teach him to lead in hand and to stand still while you mount or, better still, vault on, and you will be winning red rosettes.

SACK RACE. Competitors usually start at the far end of the ring. On the starting signal, they gallop half or a third of the way down, dismount, grab a sack, get into it and race past the finishing line leading their ponies. You need a sensible pony for this competition. It can be practised on the lawn at home without a pony. Practise getting into a sack then hopping or running in it, whichever you find easiest, holding the sack in one hand. When you can do this easily, practise with your pony in the other hand. Practise jumping off at a canter, too.

APPLE AND BUCKET RACE. Competitors will be expected to gallop to the other end of the ring, dismount, kneel down and remove an apple from a bucket of water with their teeth, remount and probably gallop back with the apple still in their mouths (though rules tend to vary in this competition). If you have sticking-out teeth you may be able to nudge the apple to the side of the bucket and then plunge your teeth into it. Otherwise, plunging your head to the bottom of the bucket is probably the best tactic in this race, though you may have to remove your hat. Practise getting an apple out of a bucketful of water at home, make sure your pony does not mind dripping hair, and you should have a fair chance of winning.

RUN AND LEAD. There are variations of this race (Run, Mount and Gallop, for instance) but at most gymkhanas you will simply gallop to the far end of the ring, dismount at a marked spot and run back leading your pony. The first

12

runner and pony across the line wins. Your pony needs to lead freely to do well, and you should be able to leap off while he is moving and then run. The faster you run, the more likely you are to win.

POTATO AND BUCKET RACE. Helpers are sent to the far end of the ring to hold the potatoes. At the other end is a line of buckets, one for each competitor. When the flag drops, you gallop to the far end, collect a potato, gallop back and put it in your bucket. Usually there are three potatoes. The first rider to get three in the bucket and raise an arm to tell the judges is the winner. Anyone who misses the bucket must dismount, pick up the potato, remount and throw it in the bucket. If you cross lines or knock over the potato holders, you are liable to disqualification. Occasionally, the potatoes are placed on poles instead of being held by helpers. You can practise this event at home using stones instead of potatoes. If you have no assistant, or poles, use a gate or wall, or two buckets upside-down on top of each other.

BENDING RACE. Poles are placed in straight lines 24 to 30 feet apart. There are usually five or six in a row, with four to six rows. Starting at one end of the ring, you gallop in and out of your line of poles, round the top and back. If you knock down a pole you are disqualified; if you miss one out you can go back and round it and still win your heat. You need a fast handy pony for this event. It can be practised at home, if you have suitable poles. An unschooled pony will find bending difficult, so start practising at a trot and concentrate on a close turn at the top. Then, when he can do this easily, start cantering and finally do it at a gallop.

A good turn at the top and a fast gallop back are of great importance in this race.

MUSICAL POLES. There is always one pole fewer than the number of riders in this competition. The poles are placed in the middle of the ring. Competitors gallop round the edge, keeping outside markers, which are usually jump wings. When the music stops or a car hooter is blown they gallop into the centre and grab hold of a pole – the rider without one is then sent out. Gradually there are less and less competitors, until finally two are left. They are then sent different ways round the ring. At a suitable moment, the music stops and they gallop in to fight over the last remaining pole. If anyone carries a pole away with him he can be disqualified. If a pole is knocked down, the first dismounted rider to stand on it wins.

Some ponies love musical poles. Others are too nervous to face the scrum. You can practise at home, galloping alone for a solitary pole, or with friends and a transistor radio. Ride fast round the markers, slow when you are near a pole. Concentrate on the poles, never bunch up, choose your pole and ride for it.

TROTTING RACE. This race is often held round a ring – where the inside competitor has the advantage. Sometimes you may simply trot up to the end of the ring and back. If your pony breaks into a canter you must turn a circle before going on.

Fast trotters are usually born rather than made, but you can practise trotting fast at home. Let your pony lean on the bit, i.e. go on his forehand rather than back on his hocks, and keep rising. Practise round the field and round a pole and back. Try him against friends. Never lose your temper if he canters, just turn a circle and make him trot again.

WALK, TROT AND CANTER RACE. This is usually a race for the tens and unders. You walk down the ring one way, trot back, and finally gallop down again, past the winning post. If you trot when you should be walking, or canter when you should be trotting, turn a circle or you will be disqualified. Use each leg in turn to make your pony walk fast, and give him a loose rein. Practise a quick turn round at home.

EGG AND SPOON RACE. In this race you usually ride up the whole or part of the length of the ring carrying a spoon. You then pick up a china egg and ride back with it. The egg must be carried on the spoon and stay there without any help from your thumb. You need a firm hand for this and a steady pony. Like most events, you can practise on the lawn at home, first without your pony, and then later, mounted. You can use a round potato or a pebble for practising.

WATER CARRYING RACE. There are usually two buckets provided for this race – one empty and one filled with water – and the water has to be transported from one to the other by carton or mug. The first competitor to fill the empty bucket to a certain level wins. A quiet pony is an obvious advantage in this race. Teach yours to stand still with slack reins. Learn to ride in one hand and make sure he does not mind a wet back. Nervous, excitable ponies rarely win this race.

LITTER RACE. A number of Squeezy bottles or something similar, with their tops cut off, are used for this race. A certain number have to be picked up by a mounted rider with a cane 3–4 feet long, carried to a litter bin and dropped in. If a bottle is dropped on the way, you must pick it up again with the stick without dismounting. The first competitor to put all the bottles in the bin wins. You may also be asked to gallop across a finishing line. Practise carrying a stick on your pony before you start picking up bottles.

17

GRETNA GREEN RACE. You will need a partner. One of you must stand at the far end of the ring while the other gallops up leading the spare pony. The dismounted rider then mounts and you both gallop back over a jump, holding a baton between you. If you let go of it, you must go back and jump the fence again. You must both cross the finishing line holding the baton. There are many variations of Gretna Green Races – this is one of the simplest.

Practice makes perfect in this race – a pair who have practised at home are likely to beat a scratch pair made up on the show ground. Your ponies should like each other if they are to go well together and one should lead in hand easily. Vaulting on rather than mounting will also improve your chances.

MUG RACE. In this event you are expected to put mugs or cartons on the tops of bending poles. The competitor who puts the required number on first wins. Somebody will hold the mugs for you, as in a potato race. It doesn't matter which pole you use first. A tiny pony is at a disadvantage here, as you may not be able to reach the top of the pole without standing in your stirrups. Practise at home, but use paper cups rather than your mother's best tea service.

ROUND THE WORLD RACE. Another competition suitable for small riders. You simply ride up the ring, stop at a required place, take your feet out of your stirrups and go round the saddle once, in a complete circle. Then pick up your reins, put your feet in your stirrups, if you need them, and gallop back past the finishing line. Ponies are held for this race while you go round, so it helps if you choose someone your pony likes (some ponies hate tall men, others behave better

for grown ups than for children). Practise going round the world at home with someone holding your pony. You need to be both supple and confident for this race and preferably able to ride without stirrups, and have a pony that will stand quietly.

RELAY RACE. This can take many forms. It can be a bending relay, just an up-and-back race, or relay jumping. There are usually three members in a team and baton passing is all-important. The one receiving the baton should be positioned for a quick getaway, but must be able to stand still long enough to accept it. The team's tactics need to be planned, so decide which hand will pass the baton to which. Again, practice at home always helps. Find which ponies go best together and put the fastest and most impatient last, because he won't then have to pass the baton.

HANDY HUNTER COMPETITION. A race against time. Each competitor completes a set course alone, timed by a stop-watch. The fastest round wins, through it should be a clear

round with every task completed. You may be asked to jump several jumps, carry a sack full of straw or a mug of water from one place to another, open a gate, perhaps undoing a chain, ride through and shut it again or take down a rail, lead your pony over and replace it. In fact, do anything a handy hunter should be able to do in the hunting field! Practise all these things at home. Time yourself and try to beat your own time. This is a race almost anyone can win with practice and quick reactions.

There are many other races and competitions at gymkhanas. I have simply described the most usual. You might also compete in Balloon Bursting races (you need a quiet pony for these!), Rope Races, Dressing Up Races, Saddling Races. If in doubt, ring up the secretary of the show and ask about the rules, for there's nothing like practising a race at home before you compete.

The Prince Philip Team

This is a national competition for gymkhana ponies and riders, and the events differ from year to year. There are five riders in each team and one reserve rider. You need a nippy pony and there *are* age limits. Four-year-old ponies cannot compete, nor can fifteen-year-old riders. There are also weight limits for ponies, so, if you weigh ten stone, don't expect to compete on a thirteen-hand pony.

Some teams start training during the winter months. The first official competition takes place in April and is called the Regional. It can be far from home. If you get through the Regional, you will have to go on to the Zone, which takes place in the summer. If you win, you will go on to the Finals at Wembley in October. You will need time off from school for this and will have to compete on several days.

At all competitions your pony and tack will be inspected, not to mention yourself! Your tack must be sound, with no rotting stitches, and it must be clean and properly adjusted. Your stirrups must fit your feet. If your saddle presses on your pony's withers, or you are wearing strap shoes, or your pony has loose shoes or risen clenches, you will certainly be disqualified. So watch it! Get your trainer or an expert to check everything days before the competition, so that things can be repaired or adjusted in time.

There are rosettes for the best turned out team, so see that your pony is clean and well trimmed. Check whether the other ponies in your team are being plaited, or are wearing fancy nosebands. You will probably be expected to compete in a white shirt, whatever the weather, though you can wear what you like underneath. Your jodphurs should be clean and loose enough to allow you to vault comfortably, your long or short boots clean, your Pony Club tie clean and pressed, your badge polished. If it's cold, wear gloves until the last moment, because numb hands are not much good at carrying eggs and spoons, etc. Have someone with a mackintosh or coat to put over you when you come out, because chattering teeth are not much good either.

Don't be nasty if someone lets down the team, or drops the egg time and time again, or fails to vault, or knocks down a pole in the bending race – after all, it could be you next time, and no one likes letting their team down.

Showing

An untidy rider and pony are unlikely to win a showing class, so, if you are the sort of person who hates tack cleaning and grooms as little as possible, showing is not for you – unless you have a parent ready to slave for you, or a groom, of course!

A pony needs to be plaited for nearly all showing classes. He needs a pulled tail for some as well, and good tack. You should be properly turned out, with a dark coat, clean boots, gloves, and a hairnet if your hair is long, unless you wear it in plaits. Boys' hair should not be on their collars, either.

Your pony will need to be well-groomed and preferably stabled. He should be fat and round but not soft, which means regular exercise and plenty of hard feed. He should be well-shod with his feet oiled and in good condition. And, most of all, he should be suitable for the class in which he's entered. A round sensible pony is more likely to win a Family Pony class than an ordinary showing class. He may have to be ridden by two members of the family for this and should be able to jump a small fence. You may be asked to demonstrate his quietness, so prepare some sort of show, like crawling under his stomach, vaulting on and off and going round the world.

If you have a slightly more light-weight pony which jumps, a Working Pony class might suit him. Once again, turnout counts. If you enter a Working Hunter class, you may be expected to ride in a double bridle. This class can be great fun with a pony which jumps well but isn't quite up to ordinary jumping classes.

Don't expect to do well every time. Much depends on the judge's opinion, particularly in Family Pony classes. Teach your pony to lead in hand, school him at home, turn him out as well as possible and ride him as best you can, and if you are put in the back row don't be downhearted, you may do much better next time.

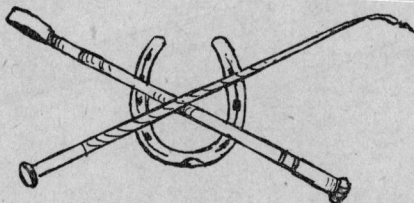

Show Jumping

Show jumping classes vary enormously, from a minimum class for under tens with jumps one foot six high, to Junior classes where the jumps can be four feet high and the spreads colossally wide. You should always arrive in time to walk the course. If your pony is inexperienced, compete in a Novice class, or, if there is one, something like a First Ever class for riders who have never won a rosette in any type of jumping competition.

There may be as many as sixteen jumps in a competition, including combinations, i.e. jumps close to one another with space for your pony to take one or two strides in between, or possibly none at all. If you jump a clear round, be prepared for a jump-off. The jumps will probably be raised and, depending on numbers, may or may not be against the clock, when the fastest clear round wins. For this, corners must be cut as much as possible, and even a fast dash through the finish can save valuable time. This is a competition where you need dash and courage, and a well-balanced pony. Lots are usually drawn to decide who goes first. If you are drawn among the last to go, watch the other competitors, compare their times, learn from them which corners to cut. If everyone knocks down a fence, you can ride for a steady clear. If they're all clear you must go for speed.

If you want to reach the top in show jumping you will have to go to shows recognized by the British Show Jumping Association, which means joining it and registering your pony. But if you're just in it for fun, you can jump at small shows, which are less formal and have smaller prizes.

Rules are much the same for all shows; three refusals (including run outs and circling in front of a fence) mean elimination. You can also be eliminated for starting before the bell, for leaving the ring before you have completed the course, for missing out a fence, for taking the wrong course, for not going through the start and finish signs, or for riding over a knocked-down jump before it has been properly put up again. (For more rules, see the Appendix.)

You can learn a lot about show jumping by watching famous riders in action. Watching them on television will teach you a great deal. Going to shows as a spectator can teach you still more. Most large towns have a show nearby every year, and there is a list of some of the famous ones in the Appendix.

If your pony is to jump well, he must be well fed and fit. You must be able to school him over painted jumps, and also round a school, because a good jumper should have his head in the right place and be obedient (famous German horses are a perfect example of this). You must ride well too, because a sudden jerk in the mouth or a loss of balance on your part can mean a knocked-down fence.

If the weather is wet or the ground very hard and slippery, your pony will need to wear studs. For this, holes must be

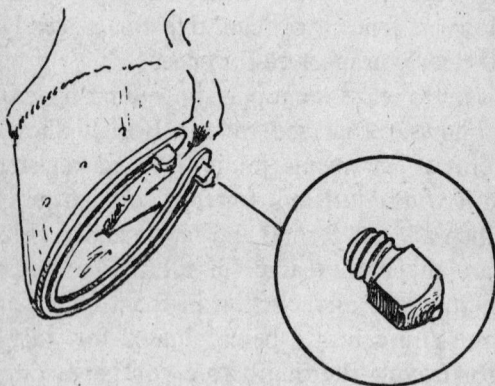

made in his shoes by your blacksmith and studs should be screwed in when you reach the show. They should never be worn on roads or lanes and, when not in use, should be kept well greased with oil or Vaseline. You will also need a jumping saddle, with forward cut flaps and knee rolls to help keep your legs in the right position.

SHOW JUMPING TEAMS. Schools sometimes organize these and there is a famous competition for the best national school team at Hickstead in Surrey. If lots of your schoolfriends ride, you may be able to get up a team, but remember that the course is likely to be large, with plenty of spreads. Pony Clubs have jumping teams, too, and, if you think you are good enough, ask your Secretary if you can be considered as a possible member.

Other jumping events held frequently are: Bareback Jumping, which is like an ordinary jumping event except that you compete without a saddle; Chase-Me-Charlie, in which you follow each other over one or more jumps which are gradually raised, and where a knock-down or a refusal means elimination; Gambler's Stakes, when you choose your own course, jumping as many jumps as you can within a time limit, higher and more difficult jumps giving you more points than easier ones – sometimes these jumps are identified by playing cards, the more difficult ones being marked by Kings and Queens and so on; Pair Jumping, which can be judged in numerous ways, the most common being that the fastest pair to go clear win.

Jumping classes are mostly decided by your age and/or size of pony, or sometimes there are local classes, for riders living within so many miles of the show, or Novice classes, which depend on what horse, or rider, or both have previously won. In B.S.J.A. jumping, the classes are divided into Grades, and a list of each pony's winnings is kept at headquarters. When your pony has won a certain amount he is automatically upgraded to the next grade.

Horse Trials and Hunter Trials

Both these competitions call for a bold pony with scope.

HORSE TRIALS. Horse Trials combine dressage and jumping and sometimes a ride along miles of tracks and roads as well. You need a really fit pony for Horse Trials and it is helpful to attend a few as a spectator before you actually compete. You will then know whether your pony is capable of getting round a course. They are run in three sections: dressage first, then cross-country, and finally show jumping. Time is often all-important. Fences are solid and a proper helmet should be worn – and these are expensive. Your pony should be able to ford a river, jump a bank or water, and be easy to ride among trees.

Your Pony Club will probably run some Novice Horse Trials and, if you attend rallies regularly, you should be able to get considerable help before you enter your first one. There are also Pony Club Team Events.

Horse Trial events are judged differently to most other competitions, including the show jumping and the dressage. Dressage marks are usually pinned up outside the secretary's tent or horse box during the morning so you have an idea of how well you are doing. The most famous Horse Trials last three days and some can be seen on television. For details of the best known and methods of judging, see the Appendix.

HUNTER TRIALS. Hunter Trials are less serious than Horse Trials, and often the jumps are no more than two feet six high. Enter for some before you try Horse Trials. They will be a good school over fences for your pony and will help to get him fit. Most Hunter Trials are advertised in *Horse and Hound* and usually in local papers.

Try to arrive in time to walk the course and don't expect even a fit pony to go round more than twice in one day. Competition is fierce at most Hunter Trials. One class can last for three hours or more and a clear round is rarely enough to win. You must go round fast and in good style to win even a fourth rosette. Because of this, most riders go for the ride rather than for prize money.

Dressage

Dressage really means 'training'. A dressage pony is a well-trained pony, and if yours isn't already schooled, you must school him. He must be able to lead off on either leg, to change from one pace to another without putting his head down, sticking it up, or pulling. In fact, all his movements should be smooth and flow into each other. Corners must not be cut and, when your pony halts, he must stand straight with his legs evenly distributed, not spread out all over the place. And his head should be in the right place too.

But don't be too disheartened by this. Other people have their difficulties as well as you, and any reasonable pony should be able to do a simple dressage test eventually. Most tests have to be learned first, though sometimes, in small competitions, movements are called.

Learning a dressage test takes time. Practise it in bits and occasionally altogether. But don't keep on riding a whole test or your pony will soon know it better than you and start doing everything before he should. If you are ambitious, mark out your dressage arena with tin cans with letters painted on them and put an X in the centre painted in white.

Never be upset about the comments the judge may write on your dressage sheet. Real dressage riders spend a great deal of time schooling. Most of them have an expert to help

them, and if you really mean to be good you will need some expert help too, but it's all the more credit to you if you ride a good test without.

Start by entering tests just for fun, and if your pony takes you out of the arena half way through, or you forget the test, remember that most people start that way and most survive and go on to do better next time. Your Pony Club secretary should be able to supply you with test instructions.

COMBINED TRAINING. This is a combined dressage and jumping competition, and a good one for a reasonably-schooled pony who isn't quite up to jumping the three clear rounds, the last at breakneck speed, which are usually necessary to win a jumping class. Your jumping marks and dressage marks are added up and the best combination wins, but do remember that in Combined Training the marks are different to those for show jumping.

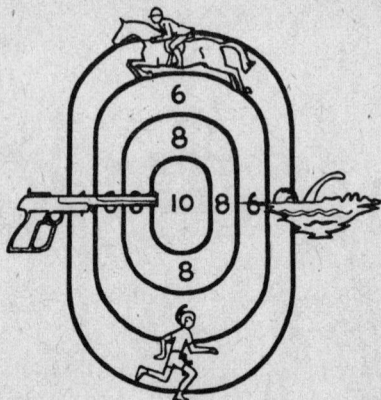

THE PONY CLUB TETRATHLON. This competition is not unisex so, if you are a girl, you cannot compete. This is, of course, very unfair because girls can shoot as well as boys, not to mention run, ride and swim!

Horses can be of any size or sex. But they must not be under five years old, nor have been Grade 1 horses for Combined Training, nor have won a Horse Trial during the current or previous year. They must also have been regularly ridden at Pony Club rallies by a member of the Pony Club (which means you can't pinch your big sister's Badminton horse and take it along). Two riders can, however, share one horse, which makes things easier if you have no pony of your own, or if yours won't jump more than one foot six or is 'gone in the wind' or getting very old.

In the riding section of the competition you will be expected to compete a course of about one mile, with sixteen to twenty obstacles, one of which will be a gate you must open and shut mounted; and another a slip rail, which has to be taken down and replaced dismounted. The obstacles won't be higher than three feet three inches, but there may be spreads, with a ditch or stream up to six feet wide. However, unlike show jumping, you *can* go past a jump and continue if you refuse three times. But this only applies to four obstacles, refuse more, and you are eliminated from the riding part of the competition.

As well as riding across country, you will also have to run up hill and down dale for some two miles, attempt to swim for four minutes without stopping and shoot at a target with a pistol, aiming for the bull's-eye. But if you're a tough person, a good cross-country runner, a fair shot, capable of swimming, and can also ride, a tetrathlon is definitely for you, though bear in mind that most of the competitions last all day and that your pony needs to be sensible as well as a good jumper.

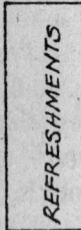

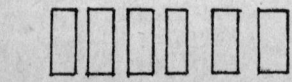

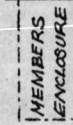

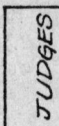

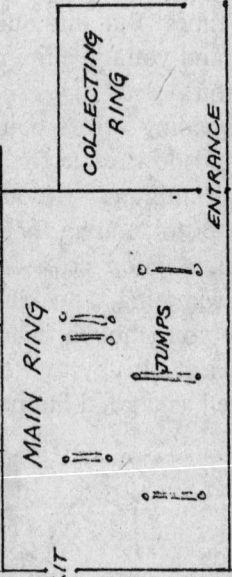

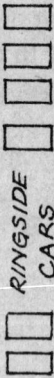

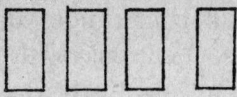

Running Your Own Horse Show and Gymkhana

Obviously, the smaller your first show, the easier it will be to run. Just a few friends with home-made rosettes and Smarties as prizes. But if it's held in àid of something, don't make it *you* – spectators might not think you a worthy cause! The R.S.P.C.A. is always in need of funds, so is the Riding For The Disabled Association, and so are Homes for Old Ponies and dozens of other societies. Or don't have it in aid of anything – let it be free, just for fun.

You will need some helpers. A judge is very necessary and, if you are competing, don't ask a relation – it's difficult enough running a show *and* competing without having Daddy judging you, which will certainly cause trouble with the other competitors if you win. Try to pick an outsider to judge, preferably someone who knows the rules. Or, better still, have two people.

You will need someone with a loud voice to organize the competitors, or they will be jumping the jumps before the show has started. A collecting ring steward collects the riders together before each class and sorts them out. If you have a megaphone let him have it.

Try and choose a flat field for your show. It needs to be at least three acres in size, much more if you are going to have 50 or more ringside cars. Ring ropes are necessary if you are expecting a lot of spectators, otherwise wild ponies may knock over push-chairs, or tiny tots, or old people. Nobody should be allowed to stand near the ring exit, as ponies can and do come out of it flat out.

Choose your events to suit your friends, your funds, your jumps, etc., and your organizing ability. Bear in mind, too, how good your competitors are likely to be. Ponies tend to become excited at shows and a Walk, Trot and Canter race is totally unsuitable for some children under eight, whereas a Walk and Trot race can pass off quite peacefully.

If you have a lot of kickers among your friends – I mean ponies, not people – don't have Musical Poles or Sack races, as a kicking match could happen in the middle of the ring. A Water Carrying race isn't really suitable for children still holding on to the saddle at a trot. A Run and Lead race is better for them, with plenty of helpers around to pick up anyone who falls over.

A Fancy Dress competition is a simple event to run and anyone can ride in it, however bad. But if the competitors are young, it's usual to give each one a rosette, i.e. First, Second, Third, Fourth, perhaps Reserve, and then lots of pink Specials.

If none of your competitors can jump, have a timed Handy Hunter race instead. In this, they can do simple things like dropping a potato into a bucket, riding up a row of bending poles and leading their pony over a jump. (Somebody should be in the ring to help small riders re-mount.) The quickest round wins.

Or you can have a Handy Pony competition judged on style (you'll need an experienced judge for this), scoring points for how well a gate is opened and shut, whether a pony can back straight, turn on the forehand, and so on. Or it can be a Best Schooled Pony competition, which will get everyone schooling their ponies for weeks beforehand. Competitors can be asked to lead off on either leg, perhaps jump, rein back, and stand still to be mounted. The possibilities are endless. But once again, have a judge who has no

reason to favour anyone, and knows his job. These sort of classes usually come first; the more exciting ones later.

Entry fees can be charged, which will pay for the prizes, but if the show is tiny, the fees should be the same – about 5p a class. Rosettes can be made out of paper if you are good at that sort of thing, or a super Mum can make simple ones out of ribbon. But make sure you have enough because there may be ties and shared prizes. Have several spare rosettes in every colour and at least six Specials.

Write a long list of what you need before you embark on a gymkhana. Have entries on the field if the show is small, unless you need the money at once for prizes. You can then give each competitor something like a cloakroom ticket in

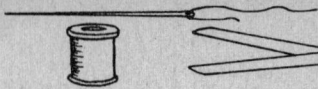
NEEDLE & THREAD

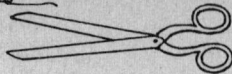
SCISSORS

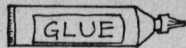
GLUE

ADHESIVE

**CARDBOARD FRONT
PAPER BACK**

TIE-ON TAPES

RIBBONS

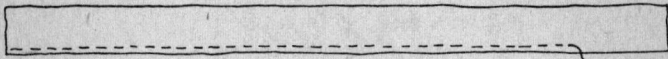
1.   **RIBBON FOR ROSETTE**

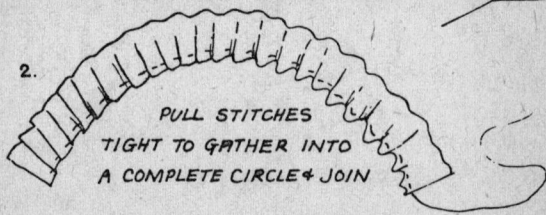
2.   PULL STITCHES
TIGHT TO GATHER INTO
A COMPLETE CIRCLE & JOIN

3.   FRONT

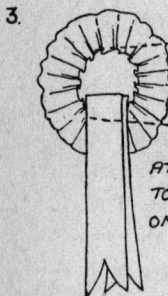 

HORSE SHOW 1st

ATTATCH RIBBONS
TO ROSETTE – GLUE
ON FRONT CIRCLE

4.   BACK

GLUE ON BACK
PAPER WITH
TAPES ALREADY
STUCK ON

5.

HORSE SHOW 1st

FRONT   BACK

FINISHED ROSETTE

exchange for his entry money, which he gives to the collecting ring steward before going into the ring to compete.

Rope can be difficult to find. If it's a small show, try to have your ring in a corner fenced on three sides; this will save both rope, posts, and work.

Buckets are easy to find. Sacks become scarcer with each passing year. Bending poles must stay up, not fall at every gust of wind. But jumps are likely to cause you the greatest problem. If your show is tiny you will probably have to make them yourself. Poles on buckets are fine as long as the poles are heavy enough. Brushwood should be tied firmly so that ponies don't drag it away tangled round their legs. Bales of straw are often used, but they are becoming as short as sacks these days.

An old ladder painted different colours and hung on posts with nails can make a sort of gate. An old door painted can be made to resemble a wall. A low feeding-trough can be a low jump or have a pole above it. Search your relations' and friends' properties for suitable material for jumps. A row of old suitcases is better than nothing. Have some broad fences like triple bars, a hog's-back, etc. Don't have a jump narrower than six feet unless it has large wings. A garage may be able to supply you with old oil cans, which can support poles or be made into a wall. A blanket put over a pole can make it much more interesting than having it as just another upright fence.

Start your course with a low fence. Six to ten jumps makes a good course for inexperienced riders, and make sure you get your distances between fences right, especially if you have combinations, i.e. one jump closely after another. (More about this point later.)

Prizes can be given with the rosettes at the end of each

class. But if you are having prizes in kind – brushes and tins of saddle-soap and so on – it may be more fun to have a prize-giving at the end of the day, with the owner of the field, or the vicar or your headmaster to give away the prizes. This is the time for votes of thanks, if you're brave enough to give them. Perhaps someone has provided teas to raise funds, or the local saddlery shop has given prizes.

Finally, if you find *you* are winning all the prizes, withdraw from further events. I once went to a party where my brother won every prize but one, which I won. Needless to say, we were never asked again. It's bad manners to win *all* the prizes at any small, invitation show, but even worse to do it at your own. At Hickstead or The Royal Windsor Show things are a bit different, of course!

A TYPICAL JUMPING COURSE

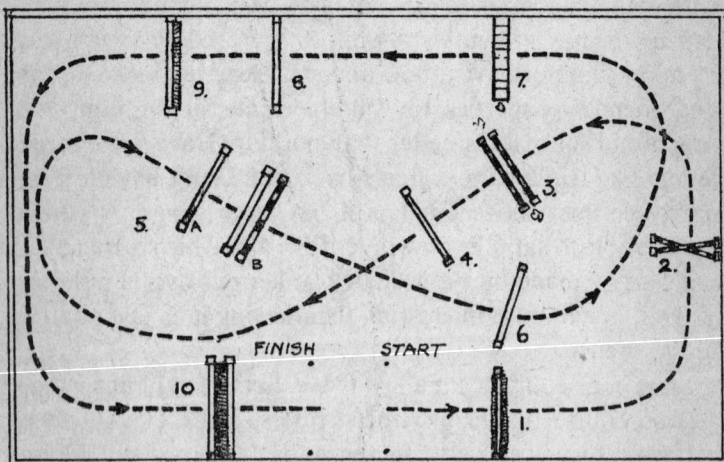

1. BRUSH + RAILS	6. GATE
2. CROSSED POLES	7. WALL
3. OXER	8. GIVE BARS
4. UPRIGHT	9. RUSTIC
5. A UPRIGHT	10. DOUBLE OXER
B OXER	

Running a Larger Show

It's best to seek some adult help for this – depending on your age. Start your preparations in plenty of time. Six months before is none too soon. You will probably need to insure competitors – horse and human – and spectators, in fact probably almost everybody and everything. A lot of horse boxes will be going in and out of a field, perhaps on to a busy road, so the police should be informed. Book your field first and remember that you will need a water supply for the horses and plenty of parking room for ringside cars. Then book judges for the jumping. Jumps can usually be hired along with ropes, stakes and perhaps even loos. Inform your local Pony Club secretary, then he or she will, with luck, put your show on the fixture card going out to all members. Order your rosettes and numbers in plenty of time, at least six weeks before you need them. (You can find suppliers advertising in *Horse And Hound* magazine.) You may be able to get loudspeaker equipment free. Consult other show organizers as soon as possible for helpful advice and suggestions. Advertise your show in the local press.

Get your schedule printed in good time. Study other schedules and get all the details right. Clauses accepting no responsibility for accidents and the right to limit entries are both important. So is the address and date of the show and the name of the secretary. First and second prizes should be larger than the entry fee. If you can, get sponsors to give money for prizes in certain classes, and/or cups. Put their names on the schedule and let them present their prizes if they are that way inclined.

If you are having competent riders, your jumps must be reasonable – poles on oil cans and old suitcases simply aren't good enough for semi-professionals and you won't enjoy running the show if you hear them complaining in loud voices all the time! Your combination fences should be 18 or 21 feet apart, but try to get a course builder to check over your course the night before, or before the show begins. Any good judge will do this, or anyone who jumps regularly in shows may be able to help.

Make your rings big enough, 80 yards by 60 yards is not too large. And try to have a blackboard outside the jumping ring so that the collecting ring steward can put up a list of numbers giving order of competing. Limit your numbers in the jumping classes. More than thirty or forty in a class is usually too much. After all, you want to end the show before midnight. Put something to this effect on your schedule and then, on the day, have a large notice outside the secretary's tent informing competitors which classes are closed for entries.

44

Make a long list of things you need. Something like this:

THINGS AND EQUIPMENT

Rosettes and numbers

Loudspeaker system

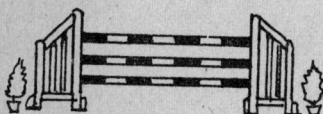

Jumps

Ring ropes, posts, etc.

Signs of all kinds – Parking, Water, Horse Boxes, etc.

Somewhere for the secretary to work; a trailer, caravan or tent will do (a car isn't really large enough)

45

Somewhere for the jump judge to sit. Table and chairs will do if it's fine, and not too hot, especially with an awning above. Otherwise, have a car with good visibility, or a caravan. Other judges can judge standing up.

Props for the gymkhana events, i.e. bending poles, buckets, eggs and spoons, etc. Make a separate list of these.

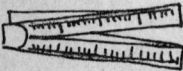

Measuring tape for jumps

Stakes, or somewhere to tie up ponies for people without horse boxes

A bell

One or more stopwatches

Paper and pens

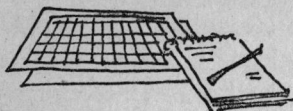

Spare schedules and entry forms

Drinks and food for the judges (but go easy on the booze if you don't want anyone seeing double!)

Some form of music if you are having Musical Poles (though a car horn will do)

Prizes. Money should be put ready in envelopes, marked with the class number and First, Second, Third or Fourth

Other prizes should have labels attached. Silver cups should be kept locked up somewhere until the last minute, or under guard. Tick everything when acquired and tick again when delivered to the field. Have receipts ready to sign for riders receiving cups. Be businesslike.

47

Judges: decide how many you need – preferably two to deal with the jumping, though one needn't be so expert but should be able to handle a stopwatch. One judge and two or three good stewards should be able to cope with the gymkhana events.

And one judge should be able to manage the Clear Round Jumping classes and a Handy Hunter competition. You will need a competent and experienced judge or judges for showing classes, but any two people can judge Fancy Dress – they need not be horsy at all.

Collecting Ring Stewards. You will need one for each ring.

Commentator. He should be experienced and put near the jump judges.

Chief Steward. One for each ring, preferably with several helpers to put up fallen jumps, and see that rosettes go in at the right time, and to help run gymkhana events.

Secretary. To give out numbers and take late entries, etc. Also to do the donkey work beforehand.

Secretary's Helper. To assist on the day.

Stewards. The more the better. To generally assist everyone anywhere.

People on the Gate. At least two, taking money, and also to help get stuck trailers out of mud.

Man With Tractor. Only if the weather is likely to be bad to pull out horse boxes and cars.

Ambulance and *Attendants*.

Veterinary Surgeon and *Doctor*. On call, or better still, on the spot.

Workers. To prepare the show and clear up afterwards.

Have everything possible put up the night before, but don't leave prizes overnight in the secretary's trailer – they might be stolen.

You will need at least two lists of jumping competitors. The chief steward should make a list of all winners in his ring, to be delivered to the secretary in due course and finally to the press for publication. Try and impress on him or her that these *must* be right, otherwise you or the newspaper may be besieged by angry letters or phone calls after publication.

Write yourself out a timetable and try to stick to it, but make all times on the schedule approximate only. Give the judges lunch if you can, but do try to get them back in the ring on time.

You can't plan the weather. But most shows go on regardless, though yours should be abandoned if the ground is deep in snow, waterlogged, or a thunderstorm is striking the competitors.

These are just a few things you will need to know to run a show. There are a lot more I may have missed out, like goodwill, a worthy cause which makes people want to help, a methodical mind and some experienced helpers, and of course, competitors.

Lastly, a few important things to remember about running your show.

DO start planning early.

DO advertise it – in the local press and by displaying posters.

DO have schedules printed in good time and leave them in saddlers' shops and places where people can collect them for themselves, as well as sending them to secretaries at other shows and to local Pony Club secretaries.

DO be clear on your schedule as to height limits for ponies and age limits for juveniles.

DO try and start your show punctually.

DO appreciate and be kind to your judges. Remember that they need really efficient stewards to put up jumps, etc, (nothing is worse than seeing judges having to run into the centre of the ring to put up fallen jumps. It isn't their job, or shouldn't be.) And don't expect them to judge continuously for twelve hours – it simply isn't fair.

DO leave the field as you found it – without broken glass, paper and plastic bags all over the place, all calculated to do frightful damage to animals.

DO send judges some kind of free car park badge before the show, and write them thank-you letters afterwards.

DO remember to have a practice jump, and someone appointed to stop nasty children jumping their ponies over it all day long.

DO, if possible, have a measuring stick around to settle arguments, but DO accept all Birth Certificates and Height Certificates as valid. (Novice Jumping class rules are much more difficult to enforce as competitors are liable to lie wildly in their longing to compete. Probably the best Novice stipulation is one which says a pony must not have won a prize of, say, either £3 or £5, which is more difficult to wriggle out of than a combined stipulation, i.e. 'prizes to the value of £10'.)

Lastly, DO pray for good weather, because that can ultimately make or break your show.

Running Your Own Hunter Trials

First of all, you need some land, and a father or friend who doesn't mind his ground cut up and his posts and rails smashed. Large ones are really better run by adults, but a small one run by yourself and friends can be great fun.

Judging at Hunter Trials varies. Some are judged by speed, when the fastest clear round wins. This is, of course, unsuitable for very small or inexperienced competitors, as accidents are more likely to happen and are usually worse at top speed. A bogey time can be set, which means someone is timed completing the course at a fair hunting pace – which means at a steady gallop but not flat out. If your Hunter Trials are for small ponies this should be done on a small pony, if for large hunters, on a large hunter. Once the bogey time is chosen the clear round nearest it wins.

Alternatively, it can be judged solely on style or on a combination of bogey time and style. Style means going at an even pace, jumping each jump smoothly and easily, going smoothly with your pony. Backward seats, or completing the whole course at a trot, or losing stirrups, all lose points.

Flags make a course look professional, one colour to be passed on your left all the way round, one on your right, but you can manage without them or use paper arrows instead. Each jump should have a jump judge. But, if this is impossible, you *can* manage with less, or even with one or two, as long as *every jump is clearly visible to them*. There should also be a few people appointed to stand at convenient places to help anyone in trouble.

Your fences should be strong but safe. Old bottles, tree stumps and strands of wire do not make safe landings and should be removed. Rabbit holes should be filled in, and low overhead branches cut down. Galloping uphill is easy, galloping and jumping downhill can be perilous for small, insecure riders, so build your course to suit your competitors.

You probably need at least five acres to run even the smallest Hunter Trials, but do realize that orchards are hazardous because of low branches, woods dangerous for small riders unless ridden through slowly (you can stipulate this first and then award faults for anyone riding faster than a trot

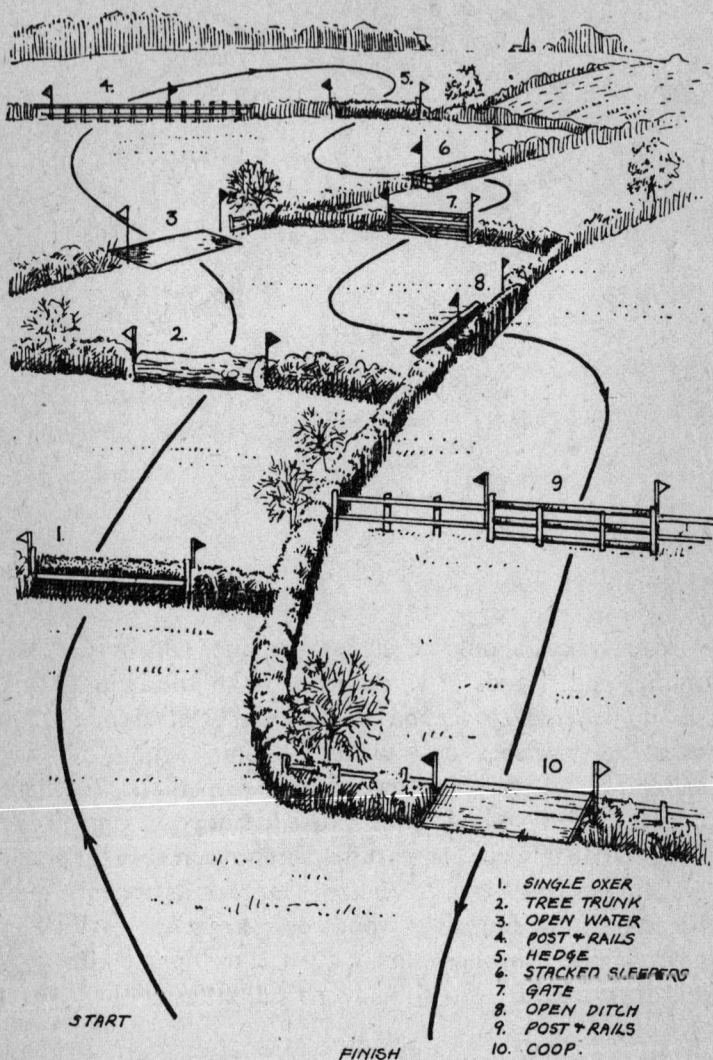

HUNTER TRIAL COURSE WITH TYPICAL JUMPS
(SHORTENED VIEW)

1. SINGLE OXER
2. TREE TRUNK
3. OPEN WATER
4. POST + RAILS
5. HEDGE
6. STACKED SLEEPERS
7. GATE
8. OPEN DITCH
9. POST + RAILS
10. COOP.

START

FINISH

through trees), and tennis lawns, golf courses and gardens definitely unsuitable, even when ridden over by only half a dozen competitors.

If you have few natural fences or ditches for your Hunter Trials, you can make a sheep pen with bales of straw and rustic poles, or dig a ditch, put plastic sheeting in it and fill it with water. But do make sure your jumps are wide enough, and that there's room to swerve on landing without running into a tree. Walk round the course imagining what could go wrong. It isn't a pleasant pastime, I know, but necessary. Any course must be rideable and safe – steep quarries must be fenced off, and any barbed wire should be some distance from jumps. Take-offs and landings must be one hundred per cent safe. And roads should be avoided altogether, even if your best friend lives on the other side and you want to use her jumps too! Lanes are all right if unsuitable for motor traffic or very rarely used. But have adults available to stop any on-coming traffic when competitors are approaching. And remember, no pony should be asked to jump on to the hard surface of a lane or, worse still, on to tarmacadam or concrete. This will soon ruin the best set of pony legs, and, if you or anyone else break their necks, it will be certainly your fault.

Pair jumping can be great fun, but do make sure your jumps are wide enough for this. Some can be taken in single file, but you should be able to jump the majority as a pair.

Many of the same rules for running a show apply to Hunter Trials. If it is large, advertise in the local press, order rosettes, numbers, etc., in plenty of time. Have stewards, judges and helpers well organized. Check everything the night before. Have hammers and nails and spare poles ready to replace any broken fences.

RUNNING YOUR OWN HORSE TRIALS. This is not really possible. Too much expert assistance is needed and many, many months of organization. Dressage judges are rare and hard to come by and jumps must be really well built. You need great experience to run anything on this scale.

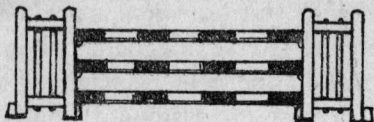

Lastly, some advice on riding in teams. These are mostly organized by the Pony Club. You may be asked to ride, or to train for a team, depending on how good you are, but either way it will take up a lot of your time. You must be prepared to give up other things if necessary. If you are already representing the county for swimming, or playing in an orchestra, or playing tennis for your school, and then going abroad for the summer, being in a team is probably not for you. But, if you have time and stamina, riding for club or school can be a great experience and, with luck, you will make friends for life. But *do* remember you may have to travel considerable distances, perhaps driven by your weary parents or in a box paid for by them, so do find out if they are keen too. Long wet days in open fields, with hours spent watching you refusing at a water jump, can be fun for you, but may not be much fun for *them*.

Sports and Pastimes including Some Strange Hunting and Pony Club Camp

Hunting

CUB-HUNTING. Cub-hunting starts at the end of the summer when the crops have been carried, and ends with the Opening Meet. Cub-hunts are not usually advertised and the meets are likely to be very early in the morning while the days are hot. Unless you are invited, always ask permission from the master to attend. Clothes are informal – ordinary hacking clothes plus a hunting whip. Ponies can be reasonably unkempt, and fitness is not very important as you are likely to spend a lot of your time standing about. If you want to be invited again, be quiet and knowledgeable.

Remember that cub-hunting is to teach young hounds to hunt, and to kill foxes. It is not organized for you to gallop madly about the countryside cutting a dash on your super new pony. The first cub-hunts will be brief, and you will probably be home in time for breakfast, feeling very healthy and unbearably superior, because you've been up for hours while the rest of the family have been in bed. If you like being up early with the birds singing and the dew still on the grass, cub-hunting is definitely for you. If you're the kind who never gets up before ten except for school, and can't be quiet, stay away.

If you *do* go, always thank the master respectfully before you leave and then ride quietly home listening to the alarm clocks ringing in still asleep houses.

FOX-HUNTING. Many people enjoy this most of all riding activities. They enjoy every moment of it; the alarm clock ringing, looking out to see what sort of day it's going to be, the early morning walk across wet or frosted grass with the first cocks crowing in the distance to find their pony, or the rush down to the stable to find him still lying down, blinking at their lantern, or the sudden rush of electric light. They enjoy grooming their pony, filled with anticipation, and the hack to the meet through the morning air, looking at weathercocks to see what way the wind blows. They enjoy the scarlet coats and the pageantry, and the long hack home when it's all over, tired but happy. To most of them, killing the fox is of little importance.

But to enjoy hunting you must know the rules. For instance, you are expected to be reasonably dressed, i.e. in riding clothes and a hard hat. You are expected to know that the hounds are called 'hounds', not 'dogs', and that there is only

one huntsman, and that the other riders in pink or scarlet coats (never red) and crash caps are likely to be officials – whippers-in, kennel huntsman, master, field master, secretary and so on. Also that the men in scarlet wearing top hats are subscribers not huntsmen. You must keep away from hounds. Keep behind the field master with the field (which isn't a stretch of green grass fenced for cows, but you and the other riders in a group). Only experts and fools follow their own line out hunting, so go with everyone else, keeping away from ponies with red ribbons on their tails, because they're kickers.

When in doubt keep your mouth shut. Talking when hounds are drawing – searching for the fox's scent – distracts hounds. Riding about on your own can head the fox, perhaps the greatest sin of all in the hunting field – this means turning him back into a wood when he was about to break into the open.

Keep your pony's head towards hounds when they pass. Keep out of their way. Be ultra polite. Opening gates for the aged, or the master, or anyone else, will make them remember you as a polite person, however shaggy your pony, long after they have forgotten the thrusters in black coats and white hunting ties. When the huntsman blows the 'gone away' – quick short notes on his horn growing longer, to many the most thrilling sound in the world – go with the others, shutting your eyes against flying mud. If your pony can't jump, get out of the way and let others have a go, or find a way round. If someone falls off, help him. If *you* fall off, be brave about it. Get on again and go on.

When hounds check, dismount if your pony is blown. Let him hang his head and get his breath, while you eat your sandwiches or talk in an undertone to friends. Remember to tighten your girths half way through the day, because ponies lose weight as they gallop and a slipping saddle is dangerous, especially when you're galloping downhill or soaring over a drop fence.

And, if your pony is unfit, go home at two o'clock or after a run has ended; but if your pony is in peak condition,

go on until the end. Then say goodnight to the master before you leave, turning your weary pony's head towards home or horse box. If it's a long way, loosen his girths and walk up the hills. If it's dark, keep to the verges and lanes. Sing as you go, it will make the miles seem shorter. And when you reach home, see to your pony first. Someone – brother, sister, parent or friend – should have made a warm mash for him, of bran and hot water, with a handful of oats, grated carrot, apple, or whatever your pony likes, added. But water him first, before he eats. Go back later and see that he is all right, go over his legs for thorns and scratches, or cuts. Remember that a deep cut may need an anti-tetanus injection so don't waste time – if he's injured, ring the vet.

A tired pony living out will roll – it's his way of having a bath. A stabled pony will need the worst of the mud brushed off when dry, but don't go on and on, because he's tired and wants to be left alone with a full net of hay and his memories.

Go out last thing and check once more that he's all right. Feel his ears; if they're icy cold, he's cold, and needs another rug. Rest him the next day, whatever happens, and never hunt more than three times a fortnight, even if your pony is clipped and rearing to go. And if you want to hunt often, you will need a clipped pony – ponies in long coats lose too much condition. After all, you wouldn't like running all day in a heavy overcoat, which is what he's wearing.

A FEW THINGS TO REMEMBER ABOUT FOX-HUNTING. You will be expected to pay 'a cap', i.e. a fee for the pleasure of hunting. Find out how much it is from your Pony Club or hunt secretary and have it ready when the secretary holds out his or her hat for it, either at the meet or at the first convenient gateway. Have exactly the right sum because the secretary won't have time to fiddle with change. And don't resent paying. Hounds cost a fortune to feed, and hunt

servants have to be paid and their horses fed. Your money is just a very small contribution.

Always remember to shut gates after you, if you are the last person through, or lost and alone, and to ride round the edges of fields with growing crops. Remember to walk through sheep, and to report any fence you have smashed irretrievably to the hunt secretary, so that the hunt can repair it. (This will be an unpleasant task, but better than a herd of cows getting on to a main road or motorway.)

Remember that a few sandwiches in your pocket should be enough for lunch. Never carry them in a satchel.

And, finally, remember that 'manners maketh man' in the hunting field, so watch yours at all times.

DRAG-HUNTING. This sport can be tremendous fun, but it is likely to be much faster than some fox-hunts, with lots of jumping. So don't embark on it until you can jump at least three feet and stay on up hill and down dale. If you dote on foxes and hate all blood sports, and love riding fast over fences, this is probably the sport for you. In drag-hunting, hounds follow an artificial scent – usually something smelling of fox or aniseed, dragged over the distance of the hunt. It can be lifted and carried to cause a check, to make the hunt more interesting, and to give the horses and riders a short rest. In this way the speed of a hunt can be decided in advance and you will never have a blank day. Drag-hunting is a marvellous way of schooling your pony to go well across country.

BEAGLING. Not for riders, but good for you. The hounds hunt hares and *you* run. It is an excellent way of discovering how your pony feels after a fast run. Try running across ploughed fields, up steep hills and through deep mud and you will learn a lot about hunting from a pony's point of view.

HUNTING WITH BLOODHOUNDS. This is now an accepted sport. It tends to be slower than drag-hunting. You may hunt a human – but not necessarily a criminal. More often you follow a trail, as in drag-hunting, and catch the trail-layer at the end. Sometimes there are three trails, each about three miles long.

HARRIERS. This breed of hound is smaller than a foxhound, and hunts hares. They tend to run in circles so that you can see quite a lot of hunting standing still on a hill top. This can be very helpful if your pony is slow or won't jump, as you are not likely to lose hounds altogether – a trying experience at the best of times.

STAGHUNTING. Most staghunting happens in the West Country. The most famous pack hunts over Exmoor, and you need a sure-footed hunter for this. The season starts in August and continues to the middle of October, and then starts again from the end of March until the end of April. This is because after October the stags are rutting and exceedingly dangerous.

Staghunts can be very fast and the stag or hind will usually finally stand at bay in a river or sometimes the sea. You need to be tough for this sport both physically and emotionally. Remember too, that if you are hunting in Devon or Ireland there are likely to be banks as well as stone walls, so you will need courage as well.

HUNTING YOUR OWN PACK OF HOUNDS. My brother thought of this when we had a couple and a half of spaniels. We ran dressed up in an odd collection of blazers, and

carrying hunting whips. But one of us ran in advance, trailing a smelly bit of meat on a piece of string. It was really a kind of drag-hunt and tremendous fun. If you have enough open space, a farm, or good friends with land, you can have your own little pack and follow on ponies. Most dogs will follow a scent and, if you and your friends have a few basset hounds between you, plus the odd beagle, you've got a pack already. But keep away from sheep, and hunt in the autumn and winter when the fields are stubble and the hay long carried. Shut gates after you, and always make sure you have permission to cross private land. Lay the trail away from roads and railway lines, and either hunt it live or soon after it has been laid. It's a lovely excuse for yelling and view hollering and you will learn something about hounds at the same time. It is surprising how well the most unexpected breeds follow a scent, giving tongue and enjoying every minute of it.

If you long to be a Master of Foxhounds, hunting your own pack is an excellent beginning and you will learn a great deal from it which could stand you in good stead later when you're hunting a real pack of foxhounds, dressed for the occasion on a large hunter – a sort of god on horseback.

Lastly, a few words before your first hunt with any sort of hounds. Please remember that:

Hounds sleep in lodges, *not* bedrooms.

They are counted in couples, *not* ones and twos.

Foxes are counted in braces – two foxes make one brace.

A father hound is called a 'sire', a mother a 'dam'.

A female fox is called a 'vixen'.

A male a 'dog fox'.

When hounds are on a scent, they 'give tongue', or are 'in full cry' (not yelping or shouting).

If someone lets out a piercing shriek, he's giving a 'view
holloa' (he's not in agony).
If he holds his cap above his head he's also seen a fox but
is being a bit quieter about it.
When a fox has 'gone to ground', he's gone down his earth
(underground home) or down a drainpipe or a hole.
To draw blank is not to find the scent of a fox.

If you use the right terms, hunting people may well respect
you. Call coats 'red', hounds 'dogs', bitches 'lady dogs', and
lodges 'hounds' beds' and they won't respect you at all, and
let's face it, we all like a little bit of respect sometimes!

A SCAVENGER HUNT. Easy to organize, this can be tremendous fun. Groups of riders compete to find a list of objects
and the first group back with all the items wins. Small
riders can be given a list of simple things to find, such as
certain flowers, a round pebble, hidden sweets or chocolate,
a piece of chalk, sheep's wool, feathers. They can have their
hunt in two or three flat fields where the ponies won't want
to start racing, and there can be plenty of helpers around to
assist competitors in trouble. If the riders are really small,
the hunt can be limited to a trot, or competitors can be led.

For competent riders, you can have much more fun with
a long list of items to find – such things as the name and date
off a tombstone written in lipstick on a paper handkerchief,
a copy of yesterday's *Times* or *Telegraph*, an old horse-
shoe, a piece of yellow gorse, a flint, a crust of bread, a
handful of oats, three matches and a bus ticket, a piece of
binder twine with nine knots tied in it – the possibilities are
endless. But do make sure all the items on the list can be

found within, say, a five-mile radius. And warn competitors of any anti-horsy people living in the area who won't enjoy a sudden rush of riders all pleading for a paper handkerchief and lipstick!

At the end of the hunt, you can award prizes and/or rosettes to the winners and finish up with a picnic, or just orange squash and buns. But do set a time limit. Give a time when everyone should be back at the starting point, otherwise competitors may go on searching for things until nightfall, exhausting their ponies and having to ride home in the dark.

A TREASURE HUNT. What treasure there is and how much
it is worth depends on the money available (unless you have a
kind sponsor who will donate it). It is usually sweets or
chocolates with something suitable for the winning ponies as
well.

The treasure hunters usually set off in small groups or
pairs. Much of the success of the hunt depends on the clues,
which can be of varying kinds. They can give directions in
rhyme, something like, 'Go to a pool, where it's cool. Look
by a tree as high as your knee'. Or there can be a sketch of
something, or even a map with clues marked on it with an
X, or words in code. What sort of clues you use should
depend on the age and intelligence of your competitors.
Remember too, that a local child will always have an advantage over others who have come by horse box, so try to put a
child who knows the district in each group.

Sometimes the competitors start with sealed notes in
envelopes, each one giving a different clue, so that the hunt

doesn't develop into a mad scramble of follow-my-leader. Sometimes bits of string or white rag are tied to trees and gateposts, to help guide competitors to clues (this is particularly helpful if competitors are small or don't know the area). With better riders, jumps can be incorporated into the hunt to make it more exciting.

The last clue can be in the form of an anagram, which must be worked out for the competitors to discover the whereabouts of the treasure. It could look something like: XOBESROH NI EHT NRAB, if the end of the hunt is at the horsebox in the barn. You need a fast, sensible pony for treasure hunts, which will tie up and stand still while you mount and dismount. Galloping madly doesn't really help, because you will probably pass the clues if you go too fast, and, if you don't know the countryside, you may also get lost. Clues can be laid the day before, but not if there are loose animals nearby who can eat them or if they are near roads or signposts where they can be removed by children. Remember too that fields should be empty of horses or they may try to join in the hunt and cause general havoc.

You need a lot of ingenuity to organize a treasure hunt. Clues written on paper should be put into plastic bags if rain seems likely. Riders should be well briefed before setting out, told where they should and should not ride, otherwise you may have eager hunters galloping across lawns and gardens, over cricket pitches and through hayfields. They should also be told to return clues once read. Someone should be available to help anyone in trouble and someone else should ride round after everything is over, making sure that all gates, etc., are shut. There should be a definite finishing time, when all competitors must be back at the start, and competitors should be counted at start and finish.

SPONSORED RIDES. If you hold a sponsored ride, you may raise a lot of money, but they can be difficult to organize. Rides are usually held over a distance of between twelve to twenty-four miles and divided into a longer and shorter section. Every rider should have a sponsor card, on which there are spaces for the names and addresses of sponsors, and how much they will give per mile. If you are riding 24 miles and someone sponsors you for 2p a mile, this means that if you ride the whole distance he should give you 48p. Friends or relations can fill up your sponsor card, or you can go begging sponsors from house to house. After the ride, you go back to the same people, with your sponsor

card signed by one of the organizers to prove that you have ridden a certain distance, and collect the money. This is usually the hardest part of the ride! Sponsored rides are often run by riding clubs or the Pony Club. Some include jumps. A few consist of a ride over jumps when you earn so much for each jump jumped. Some are advertised in *Horse and Hound* or in local papers. Prizes are sometimes given, usually to the rider with the most sponsors rather than the one with the most money. Rosettes can also be awarded.

It is important to have a fit pony for a sponsored ride, and it is vital that your card is signed at all check points and at the end. Make sure that your pony's shoes fit and are tight. And do wear a hard hat and suitable shoes. Usually riders go in groups or pairs on sponsored rides, setting off at ten-minute intervals. Try to go with ponies of roughly the same size, or one of you will be always jogging and another waiting for the others to catch up. There is not usually a set time and a steady pace is best.

MUSICAL RIDES. These are often a great end to a great day. They are sometimes held on the last day of Pony Club Camp. You can organize one for charity if you have enough friends to take part. Twelve riders is probably the minimum needed and ponies should be paired according to size and stride, and if they match in colour, too, the ride will look even more impressive. An area 60 to 80 yards long is probably large enough for twelve to sixteen riders. It is helpful if you put markers at key points round the outside, particularly at the centre of each end, and one in the middle (a painted X will do here). Work out your ride on foot first. You can obtain excellent detailed instructions on these, with diagrams, from The British Horse Society (see Appendix), or try working out

74

one on your own. Start slowly, because it is better to be successful at the trot than to disintegrate into crazy disorder at a canter. Put kicking ponies at the back and born leaders in front, but remember that the leading riders should be intelligent and know their right hands from their left. Try to wear matching outfits, and an identical buttonhole if you are wearing coats.

Choose your music to suit the tempo and speed of your ride – four-time for a walk, two- to four-time for a trot, something faster for a canter. Make sure it is loud enough to hear wherever you are in the arena.

A musical ride is an excellent exercise for you all, riders and ponies, because your pony must be under control at all times, and going in an orderly way.

Polo

No one is quite certain where this game started, but it is known to be one of the oldest in the world and was played many years ago in Persia, Northern India and China. When first played in England, it was called Hockey on Horseback and the players rode small, wiry ponies. Later, the height limit was raised to 14 hands, but in 1918 this rule was abolished and now polo can be played on horses of any size. Pony Club polo officially started in 1959 and there is now a tournament every year.

Polo is played between two teams of four riders. The ground should measure 240 by 200 yards and the goals are eight yards wide. A goal is scored when a ball passes, at any height, between the posts. A player is handicapped depending on how good he is – up to 10 goals. This does not mean he has to score or give away his handicap number of goals, but indicates how valuable he is to his team. Pony Club polo usually has two chukkas (rounds) of six minutes each, with a three-minute interval between. The game starts in the centre of the ground and there is a mounted referee. It is largely a game of attack and defence.

Before playing polo, try to learn the rules. Go and watch matches, too. These are often announced in *Horse and Hound*, but to help you further I have listed some polo grounds in the Appendix.

You need a fit, well-balanced pony for polo, behind the bit rather than on it, because most of the time you will be riding

him on a loose rein held in one hand. He should be bold as well, or he won't like riding another pony off. School him to neck-rein and turn on a sixpence. Then try dribbling a ball about at home. If you have no stick, make yourself some sort of substitute – even your mother's long-handled broom is better than nothing! The idea is to accustom him to carrying a stick before you start hitting a ball. A plastic ball will do at this stage.

As you progress, you will need more equipment, though the Pony Club may be able to supply you with a polo stick on loan. Your pony will need polo boots or bandages on his legs, a pelham or double bridle and a standing martingale. You will need a polo helmet, a left-hand glove, and later on polo boots and breeches if you wish to look the part.

More and more branches of the Pony Club are playing polo. If yours doesn't, start a pressure group. Girls can play as well as boys, so find six or seven of you who are keen, and write to your District Commissioner or Pony Club secretary asking for help.

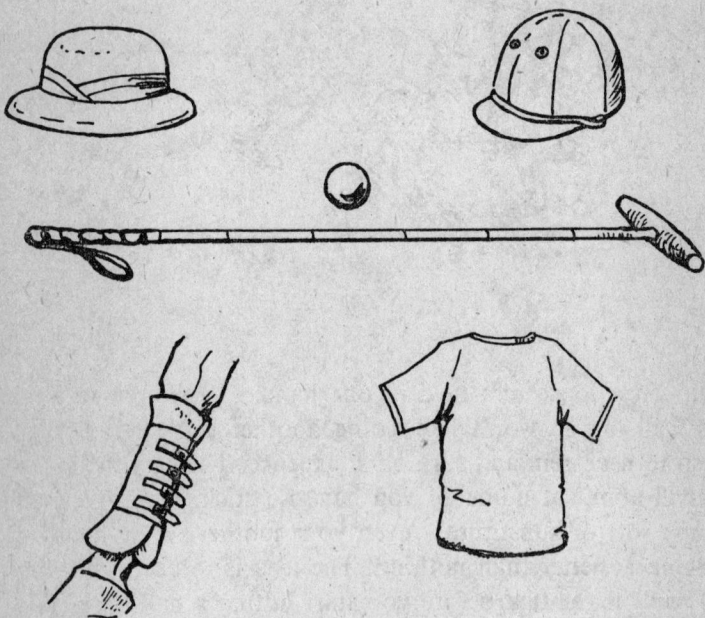

Pony Club Fixtures

MOUNTED RALLIES. Here you will learn a lot, and your pony should improve too. Appear in tidy clothes, wearing a hard hat and sensible shoes or boots. Groom your pony and clean your tack. Introduce yourself when you arrive, particularly if you are a new member. Your name should be on a list and should be ticked on arrival. Basically, you are taught horsemanship at a mounted rally. Your tack will be inspected and adjusted correctly if need be. If your pony is in bad condition you will be given good advice as to worming, calling the vet and increasing food. Don't take criticism badly, the Pony Club is there to help you. If your saddle

does not fit, for instance, the sooner you know it the better, otherwise your pony may be out of action for weeks or months with a fistulous wither or bad back. If your stirrups are too small for your feet, you could fall off and be dragged – with nasty results. All these things are important and concern your riding.

After your inspection, you will be allotted to a 'ride' and introduced to your instructor. You will then start schooling, perhaps finishing up with some jumping or mounted games.

Before you go home from a rally, always thank your instructor for the lesson, whether you enjoyed it or not. Leave the field or school quietly in an orderly fashion, and, if your saddle needs stuffing, or your pony needs new shoes, have it done without delay.

Pony Club rallies can be a marvellous way of making friends and improving your riding at the same time. Often they have the most expert instructors, most of whom give their services for nothing. So, if you want to make progress, attend as

many as possible, and remember that many of our greatest riders regularly attended rallies in their younger days.

DISMOUNTED RALLIES. At these you usually learn about stable management – feeding, grooming, rugging, bandaging, bedding, etc., and also about tack. Or you may be taken round the hunt kennels, or to see racing stables, or in a coach to Hickstead. They are usually both instructive and fun, and you and your pony will both benefit if you attend, so make the effort, and if your parents can't take you, go on your bike. Best clothes are not generally worn.

Other Pony Club functions are Children's Meets, Treasure Hunts, etc., most of which are dealt with elsewhere in this book. There is also a Quiz team or two in most Pony Clubs, so, if you are reasonably brainy and don't mind appearing in public, ask if you can be trained for one. What you learn could help both you and your pony in the long run, even if you never make the team.

PONY CLUB TESTS. D Test is quite easy. You should know some points of the horse and what the pieces of your tack are called. You should know how to catch your pony, and be able to mount and dismount, walk, trot and canter, and to lead your pony in hand correctly, i.e. with the reins over his head and his stirrups run up, and when you turn him you should push him round, not drag him after you like an unwilling dog.

But the tests do get more difficult, and if you want to pass them you must buy the recommended books, in particular *The Manual of Horsemanship*, and study the test cards, all of which are available from the secretary of your Pony Club. Don't try and take them too soon. It's better to wait six months and pass, than take one early and fail. C Test is usually taken from eleven years upwards, and B Test from fourteen upwards. They both cover stable management as well as riding, and such things as rugging and bandaging.

Taking tests is not exactly fun but you do feel you've achieved something when you pass. And, as you get older, you will find that being able to say, 'I've passed C Test', or B, or whichever it may be, is a help when borrowing a pony or getting a job.

PONY CLUB PARTIES. These usually have a distinctly horsy flavour and can be great fun. Find out what other people are wearing though – it's awful to turn up in a frilly dress or a pinstriped suit if all the others are in old jeans!

PONY CLUB CAMP. Sometimes this is residential, sometimes not. At many camps the humans sleep in tents and the ponies in comfortable, well-bedded-down stables. Food is usually super. Work is hard. Boxes or stalls must be properly mucked

out, ponies groomed and tack cleaned, and you can't leave it to parents – *you* have to do it *yourself*.

Hay is generally provided, but you will probably be expected to take hard feed. Write your name firmly on everything that's yours without fail. Wheelbarrows can sometimes be shared, so can forks and brooms, but make sure you like the person with whom you are sharing otherwise difficulties can develop!

You *should* learn a colossal amount at camp and develop some muscle. Try to put your pony next to a friend of his and remember that he will be working very hard so will need more oats, etc., than usual.

If you can't bear to leave home, you can probably go daily. There is usually an open day or gymkhana at the end of the camp so that you can show your relations how much you have improved and make them agree to you going again and again. But if you don't enjoy camp, don't feel that you are peculiar or an outcast. Lots of people don't like a communal life! It's all a matter of choice. Camp is a wonderful place to iron out any difficulties you may have with your

pony, because all the experts are there. It should improve both of you at least fifty per cent if it's your first time, and quite considerably every year in future. You may make life-long friends too. So, if you can, go at least once – after all, it's a change for your pony and we all need changes sometimes.

A few Do's and Don'ts about camp.

DON'T take your pony if he won't tie up, unless he can be turned out or live in a loose box.

DON'T take a three-year-old.

DON'T go if you hate mucking out, grooming and can't trot without holding on (unless there are special arrangements for beginners).

DON'T expect to take your groom with you.

DO take two pairs of jodphurs and everything on the camp list.

DO take medicine if you need it, and tell someone.

DO take plenty of clothes for wet weather.

DO wash occasionally, even if no one else does.

And finally, DO try to stay sober on the last night, even if there's a super party going on.

Pony Trekking

TREKKING CENTRES. A list of addresses is published yearly in *Horse and Hound*. They are also advertised in *Pony* and *Riding* from time to time. There are many pony trekking centres to choose from, and most of them provide excellent accommodation, some having tennis courts and swimming pools as well as riding facilities. Choose an approved centre and try to view it before booking. Be honest about your riding abilities and don't underestimate your weight. Book as early as possible in the year, because the best centres will be fully booked first.

Treks vary; some may consist of little more than all-day riding over hills or mountains. On others, you may ride from place to place, staying at a different one each night. All are likely to be slow, so don't expect mad gallops. Take the

recommended clothes and never trek without a hard hat, even if your leader only wears a headscarf. Take money, and extra provisions for long days out when you may become hungry with alarming frequency. Take gloves and waterproof clothing for wet days, and warm sweaters, because it can be cold even in August if you are high up. Wear suitable shoes or boots.

Pony trekking can teach you a lot and is a marvellous way of spending a holiday, particularly if you have little opportunity for riding at home. Go with a friend if you can, because it's usually more fun than going alone. Try to do some riding first, so that you are reasonably fit, and take plenty of sticking plaster for sore knees, etc.

PONY TREKKING ABROAD. This can be very enjoyable, though it tends to be expensive. Choose your centre carefully, making sure that you are capable of managing the horses provided. Trekking centres abroad vary enormously. At some you trek for miles, sleeping in a different cabin each night. At another you would explore the Camargue. In Iceland the ponies tend to be steady, placid and strong; in Hungary and Spain, they will be a different breed altogether. (For further details see the Appendix.)

LONG DISTANCE RIDING AND PONY TREKKING WITH FRIENDS. Long distance rides take a lot of planning. Before you start on a long trek, it is probably best to try a shorter distance to test your equipment. Where you go is of tremendous importance. Britain is covered with possible routes, from the Yorkshire Moors to the Sussex Downs, from mountainous Wales to bleak, boggy Dartmoor, over the Pennines, or along the renowned Icknield Way. Further

details of these routes and more information can be found in the Appendix. But do choose your routes to suit your mounts. Thoroughbreds may be happy on the Sussex Downs but find Wales unbearable. The Yorkshire Dales could need sound hocks. Dartmoor needs good compass readers and sure-footed mounts.

You can stay at hostels, trekking centres, riding schools or with friends; you can then arrange for clean clothes to be sent ahead of you and perhaps have a steaming bath at night. Hard feed can be provided for your ponies, too, and maybe loose boxes if it's wet and cold. But this will be more expensive than taking a tent. Whichever type of ride you choose, plan ahead. Buy maps and learn to map-read, and buy a compass. Leave nothing to chance. Make lists and tick off items. Don't expect to ride fifty miles in a day. Twenty miles is probably long enough for the first day, with a long break in the middle. Allow time for getting lost, and always tell someone adult and responsible exactly where you are going so that if disaster does strike you can be found easily.

For a long ride, ponies must be fit, and their tack comfortable. Feet should be well-shod, both equine and human. Elementary first-aid equipment should be carried, particularly sticking plaster and antiseptic cream suitable for ponies as well as people. If you decide to take a tent you will need cooking utensils. If you can, persuade adults to meet you at some given spot with sleeping bags, one tent or more, hard feed for the ponies, saucepan, frying pan, food, etc. Wet clothes can then be taken away and dry ones provided if necessary.

A full list of items needed is listed in *A Guide to Pony Trekking and Mounted Expeditions* (see Appendix). This includes useful things like a torch, a pen-knife, and plastic bags for spare clothes. You will need soap, too, and a tooth-

brush. A grooming kit can be shared, but each pony should have his own headcollar and rope. The headcollar can be worn under his bridle with the bridle noseband removed and the rope tied round his neck. Each pony will also need some utensil for his feed, either a cloth nosebag or, better still, a bucket.

Ponies also need somewhere to sleep, preferably a field where they can roam at leisure. Try to put friends together, but don't pitch your tent in their field, unless you want soft noses waking you in the night, or hoofs entangled with guy ropes with disastrous results. Never turn your ponies into a field without permission, or tether them to bushes or trees. If you decide to tether them, proper stakes must be brought, and they must be taught to tether before you start on your expedition.

Don't take your dogs with you, unless they are angels, because even the best-behaved dog can cause havoc on a riding holiday, stealing the sausages, chasing sheep, running out in front of lorries. They can become footsore or will disappear for hours hunting rabbits.

Ride sensibly. Mad races will tire your ponies far quicker than going at a steady pace. Always stop riding well before dark, but try to carry luminous jackets, which can be bought cheaply and worn over your clothes, for emergencies. Remember that your ponies need grazing time if turned out so do give them a fourteen-hour night if you can. Always shut gates after you, and leave your camp ground tidy without any tins, plastic bags or paper lying about. Inspect your ponies regularly for saddle or girth galls and have a night and morning foot and tack inspection. 'A stitch in time saves nine' applies here too. Don't leave anything to chance.

If anyone falls off and is obviously hurt, go for help,

leaving someone with the injured rider. Never try to get him back on the pony or drag him along the ground.

Long distance riding or trekking is the most marvellous way to spend a holiday. Plan ahead, prepare your pony, making sure he is really fit, choose your friends with care, and it can be the experience of a lifetime. Never start on unfit, lame or very old ponies. Remember to take plenty of money – for food, for sets of shoes, for emergencies. And, when everything is ready, stop worrying and enjoy the beautiful bits of Britain which most people never see, the hidden valleys and bleak mountains, the rolling downs, and the tracks which the Romans marched along so many years ago.

(For more useful details see the Appendix.)

Things to Do at Home
plus some Odds and Ends

Making Your Own Jumps

Boys are often better at this than girls, because they can usually learn carpentry or woodwork at school. But no one need despair, because using a hammer is quite easy if you don't mind an occasional black thumb nail. Or someone like your old Dad may take pity on you and help.

Jumps should be about ten feet long and poles about four inches or more in diameter, because anything less will fall too easily and make your pony careless. You can use odd bits of wood lying about your garden, if you have that sort of garden, but make sure that there are no nails sticking out. Or you can order wood from a timber merchant, but do make sure it is thick enough. (Helping yourself to trees in woods, though a cheap way out, is not really recommended). Rough poles of untreated wood can be excellent, or any reasonably thick wood. A wall can be made out of an old door with all sharp things like hinges removed. Paint rings of different colours all over it, using up the dregs of old paint pots, or make it red, white and blue one side and black and white on the other. Or better still, two doors can be sloped with a flat piece of wood along the top and a piece at each end. Four inches by four inches pieces of wood can then be used as bricks to go along the top. Poles can be painted in different colours. A long plank can be bought and painted red and white and made into a Road Closed jump.

Make a frame for a brush fence with flat pieces of wood at each end and two rails along each side, preferably three-four inches by one inch, and a flat plank at the bottom of each

side. Fill it with twigs or gorse, or even laurel, but don't leave it in the same field as your pony or he may eat it, with terrible results – possibly colic or poisoning, as well as destruction of your filling.

Don't go mad, take your time and try to make your jumps solid so that they will last. Explain to your parents that even the weediest set of jumps costs at least a hundred pounds

these days and perhaps they will help either with money or know-how. There may be an old gate lying about in an old junk yard which you can buy cheaply and paint. Old oil cans can support some of your poles, but you will need stands with feet to hang your gate on. These are never easy to make. You will need a brace and bit and some expertise. If you've got an older brother or a do-it-yourself uncle, this is

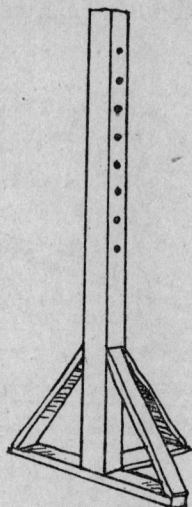

the time to seek their help. (Get your mother to invite the uncle to tea and then be plaintively struggling, and with luck he won't be able to resist helping; or bribe your elder brother.)

Once you have some good supports, everything else is relatively easy. Go round developing an eye for suitable material and you will soon have a course of jumps which may look a little odd but will serve its purpose. Then, if you are ambitious, try your hand at making cavalettii, which need solid centre poles and to be screwed or bolted together, rather than nailed, on to crossed ends. These can be used endlessly for hog's-back triples, grids, and so on.

Use your imagination and paint everything. Don't let your field resemble a junk yard. Tin cans painted red, white and blue can look marvellous, rusty and dented they are just old scrap lying about a field, hated by neighbours and country lovers alike.

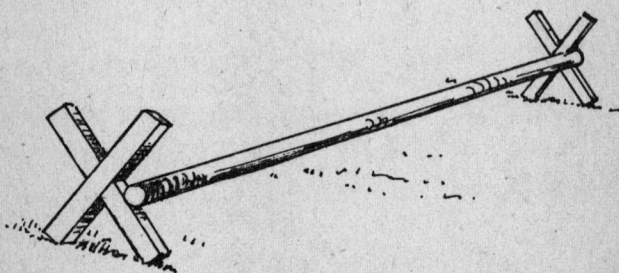

Improving Your Stable

Choose your stable colours – blue and yellow, purple and
green, anything you like – and then paint your wheelbarrow,
buckets, fork and broom in them. Stables need re-painting
from time to time as well. If yours is a creosoted loose box,
try re-creosoting it, and paint the windows and door in your
own colours, if your parents agree. A tack room can be
made quite homely with a bit of imagination. Saddle racks
can be painted exotic colours, posters put up, even your own
favourite pop star. But make sure that the paint won't come
off on the tack – a purple lining on a saddle might look a
bit peculiar and a pink bridle even worse! Keep lead paint
away from your pony – it can be deadly if licked constantly.
So put all empty paint tins into your dustbin without delay.

Your pony's name on his loose box door looks smart. You can order a nameplate or make one yourself and screw it on.

Concrete buildings can be Snowcemmed in a variety of pastel shades. A basket of geraniums can be hung on the stable wall – outside, not inside, of course. All this will make your stable look posh and original, and your tack room so nice that you can use it as a refuge from the rest of the family on occasions when you suddenly hate one another, which, let's face it, happens to most of us at some time or other.

Finally, a few Do's and Don'ts about your improvements.

DON'T paint the inside of feeding and drinking utensils.

DON'T paint haynets.

DON'T paint your father's wheelbarrow without his permission (he may not want a striped one, or whatever you have in mind!)

DON'T paint your tack. Dyeing rugs isn't really recommended, either, as they are liable to shrink.

DO paint brushes if you want to, but not the bristles.

DO creosote or paint the gate (with permission, of course).

DO paint your trailer on the outside because if it's wood it will preserve it. But don't paint Dad's car to match – he might not appreciate it.

Tack Cleaning

If you really hate this chore, you can still make it more enjoyable by listening to your favourite programme on the radio while you work, or have a tack-cleaning party. Three or four guests will probably be enough if you don't want to get all your cheek pieces and curb chains mixed up. If you're hard up, make your guests bring their own saddle soap and really make a day of it. Take everything apart, marking down which hole each strap was in first, clean it and then put it together, making sure that each piece is in its right place (for nothing is worse than finding your bit is on the wrong way round or your reins attached to the wrong ring, or your stirrup leather twisted round and round, when you are in a tearing hurry to get somewhere). As an added spur, you can get someone to award small prizes for the best-cleaned set of tack – but not your mother if you're competing; choose someone completely unbiased.

You can have grooming parties, too, and trimming sessions and then, if you don't know how to put on a tail bandage, there may be someone around to show you. You can all help each other, holding naughty ponies' heads, advising on how to remove corkscrews from tails and helping sort out difficulties. But keep the ponies a safe distance apart or there could be a kicking match. And don't tie them up by their reins, or to unsuitable things like motor cars, rose pergolas or the washing line.

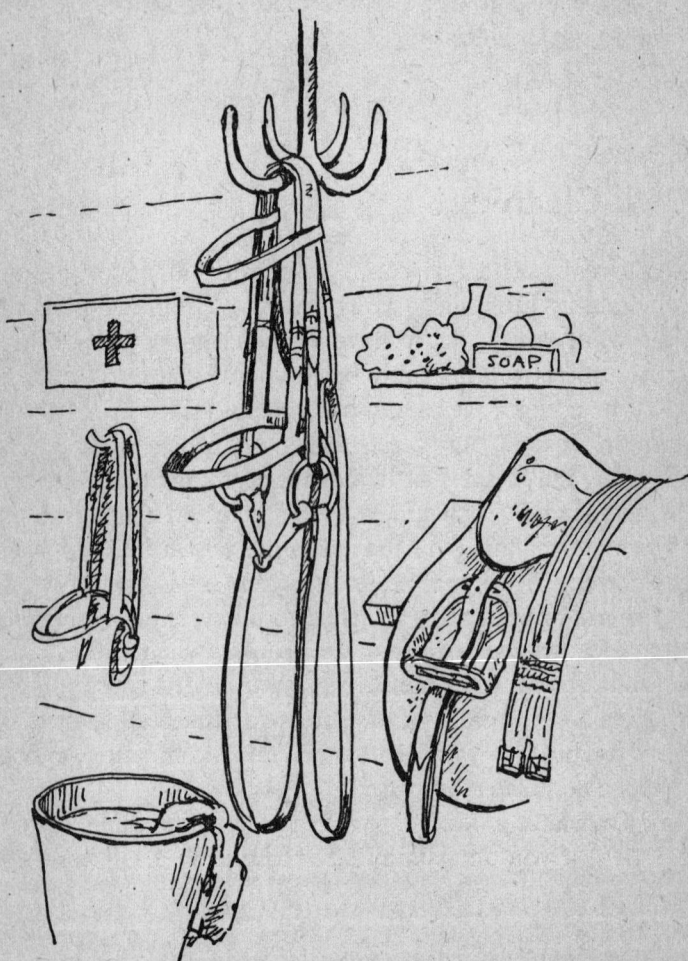

Labels on illustration: MASH, SUGAR BEET, TREACLE, SALT, CARROTS, APPLES, BRAN

Feeding

Feeding needn't be dull. Your pony likes his meals to be punctual but enjoys variety as much as you do, though he should have approximately the same amount each day. Try adding carrots and apples to his feeds (sometimes you can buy old or small ones cheaply from a greengrocer or market stall).

You can also boil his oats and make them into a pudding. Take a large saucepan and boil a pound or two slowly in water. After a short time, you will have a lovely, gooey pudding which is delicious with sugar beet added (which must already have been soaked in water for at least twelve hours), or with bran, either with a pinch of salt, or with black treacle. Boiled oats are less intoxicating than unboiled, so can be fed once or twice a week to ponies who otherwise live mainly on pony nuts, making a delicious change. But don't feed your pudding boiling hot. It should be warm to the touch, no more. A pudding can also be made out of barley, crushed or whole, in the same way. A gruel can be made out of oatmeal, or boiled linseed, but neither of these is cheap.

Nettles can be cut and made into hay, an excellent occupation when you are in a rage – thrashing nettles is much better than thrashing your pony and excellent for getting rid of frustration. Dried nettles are full of good things for your pony, but make sure you don't cut ragwort at the same time, because dried ragwort is deadly.

Grass can be cut and fed green immediately, or made into hay. But never feed grass cut by a lawnmower, because it ferments very quickly and can give your pony colic.

Teaching Your Pony Tricks

This can ruin him for ever, so *do* be sensible about what you teach. Teaching a pony to rear is sure to lead to trouble. And a bucking bronco isn't likely to find a good home if you want to part with him later on! Most circus tricks are a by-product of schooling. A really well-schooled pony can be ridden without saddle or bridle, and a really obedient pony will go almost anywhere you ask him – up steps or through fire, across rivers and over bridges. Teaching a pony to shake hands is fairly easy. Reward him every time he picks up a front hoof for you, then start tapping his elbow and saying 'Hoof'. When he moves it, reward him, until finally he will pick it up whenever you say 'Hoof'.

We once taught a pony to stand on a tub. We kept putting

one hoof on it and then one day we pulled him forward and there he was standing on it, as proud as punch. Afterwards, we taught him to wave a hoof as well. But if you want to try this, the tub must be strong and firm, and wide enough to take two hoofs. A tub which cracks or breaks under a pony's weight will terrify him for ever.

Most ponies learn tricks themselves – annoying ones, like undoing the bolts on stable doors, or opening gates. They develop strong lips to search your pockets with, and unpleasant tricks, like standing on your feet when you are doing up their girths.

Trick jumping can be great fun. We once had a competition at a local show for the most obedient pony and we used to jump one of ours over a table laid for tea and over fire. It wasn't really a trick, but what any well-trained and

sensible pony should be able to do. You can, of course, become a circus rider yourself and try to ride standing up. You need a pony with a broad back and a calm temperament. You can also lunge your pony until he learns to canter in a circle when you command, and then you can vault on and off (if you are agile enough, of course) and call it a circus trick – or just practise vaulting. None of this adds up to much; but if one of you can canter on either leg without saddle or bridle, and up bending poles and over a jump, and another can jump over fire and a tea table, and another can vault on and off either side and up over the tail, you've put together some sort of show which you can ask friends or relations to watch – for entertainment or to earn money for something or other. But do wear riding hats, disguised, if you like, with something exotic tied over them, but on your heads just the same.

104

Helping People Worse Off than Yourself

This can be very rewarding. You can give pony rides – on a pony or in a pony trap – at a fete or function for a worthy cause. But don't make the rides too cheap or you will go on giving the same children rides over and over again. 5p or 10p is not too much, and, after all, you want to stop some time. Give a time of beginning and a time of ending. Two hours is really enough for you and your pony to keep running up and down. For rides, make sure your pony's girths are tight and that the stirrup leathers go up far enough for small riders. Don't kill your pony by accepting heavy weights – set a weight limit. Take a headcollar for tying him up while you amuse yourself before going home. Make sure there is someone to collect the money; you can't manage this and be heaving riders into your saddle or helping them into a trap. Don't be *too* choosey over stirrup length, unless your pony is very tired and you want to use up time and give him a rest. Don't let riders go on their own unless they really can ride and are wearing a hard hat. And be pleased if you make a few pounds – every bit helps.

HELPING DISABLED RIDERS. This is a good idea too, and it does help some handicapped children tremendously. If your pony is very quiet and not being worked to death by you, you can offer him to a group, many of which ride only in term time, when you may not be riding much anyway. Otherwise you can help by leading a pony, or simply walking beside a child to stop him falling off. You may make friends, too.

Do remember that a disabled child needs watching – his limbs may not work very well, or he may suddenly decide to dismount for no reason at all. You must watch him all the time, so don't gossip with a friend while you are helping, or discuss his seat with the instructor. Have an eye in the back of your head for him if you're leading the pony, and keep to a steady pace. Be jolly. Riding is a day out for most disabled children and should be enjoyed, so don't keep on and on about his heels not being down or his hands being in the wrong place. Try to make his riding fun, in spite of his disabilities. (To find your local group see Appendix, or contact your Pony Club secretary, who may know.)

SHOPPING ON A PONY. If possible, go with someone else, and don't leave your pony tied up in the town car park unless he's totally traffic-proof, wearing a headcollar, and tied to something sensible. Shopping can be carried in a knapsack, or, better still, in saddle bags. Don't try to carry it in your arms or you may drop it all at traffic lights or somewhere equally disastrous. Remember to observe the rules of the road. Stop at pedestrian crossings, give hand or whip signals, don't ride on the pavement and generally give way to pedestrians. It's no good thinking you have right-of-way at every traffic junction because horses were made before cars. I agree whole-heartedly with this sentiment, but it isn't legal. If you have a friend with you, get him or her to hold your pony while you dash into a shop, but not in the main street, unless there's plenty of free parking space. Watch your pony outside greengrocers' shops or you may find yourself paying for snatched apples, cauliflowers, etc., which can be expensive.

If you have a friendly village shop, you can stand in the doorway holding your pony and ask for things, but unfortunately these sort of shops are now few and far between, and most shopkeepers don't really appreciate a pony in their shop. But shopping by pony can save your parents getting

out the car and using petrol, and will exercise you and your pony at the same time.

RIDING WITH A DOG. This is not easy nowadays. Some dogs will lead from a horse, and a few will stay to heel. But any dog which is likely to dash out from behind your pony suddenly could cause a fatal accident, so riding with even the best-behaved dog is only safe down carless lanes, across fields and through woods. Even then he will need to be under control. There may be sheep beyond a wood, which he can chase unknown to you. Or, if he's disobedient, he can disappear for ages chasing rabbits, while the hours go by and you get later and later for lunch. Probably the easiest way to manage a dog is to keep going at a steady pace, something a bit faster than a hound jog, depending on the speed and size of your dog, and in this way he will be too busy keeping up with you to disappear on some wicked pursuit of his own!

RIDING WITH YOUNGER CHILDREN OR RIDERS WORSE THAN YOURSELF. This can be nerve-racking. If you are the best rider as well as the eldest person present, you will probably be expected to take charge of the ride, and be responsible for anything that goes wrong – damaged tack, injured ponies, or even worse. If your riders are not firm in their saddles, don't gallop madly through woods or across huge fields, or they may crack their heads on trees or vanish into the distance screaming 'Help! I can't stop.' So be

sensible. Go in front, but keep looking back to see whether any pony is miles behind. If one is, stop at once and wait for him to catch up, otherwise the pony may do some catching up himself after a time, probably at a flat-out gallop with a few bucks included! Small ponies often hang back to graze on luscious grass and then catch up at full speed.

If there are rabbit holes around or low branches likely to sweep riders from their saddles, shout "Ware Hole!' or "Ware branch! Bend your head', and make sure they do.

Don't start amusing yourself at their expense. If you

intend to sail over a huge tree trunk which is far too big for your companions, be sure they are the other side first to admire your efforts; otherwise their ponies may decide to follow you, with disastrous results.

Don't expect tiny tots of six to shut heavy gates, they just aren't strong enough. If you are about to ride down a steep hill, check girths. Roly-poly ponies have roly-pony shapes and their saddles can roll round at any time. Straight-shouldered ponies with low headcarriage need special attention – their saddles can gently slide over their withers and down their necks. And, unless they are wearing a crupper, this can happen at the first steep hill you come to. Saddles slipping backwards are not impossible either, particularly if you are climbing precipices. Sliding off backwards can be very unpleasant, and stirrups banging against a pony's hindquarters can drive him mad.

On the roads, ride outside any traffic-shy pony, and slow down approaching traffic.

Riding with people younger than yourself can be boring for you, particularly if you're the galloping sort, but it may be heaven for them, so just try being unselfish for a change. After all, your pony probably needs a quiet ride from time to time and he will like the company, even if you don't.

RIDING WITH PEOPLE BETTER THAN YOURSELF. This can be nerve-racking, too. Tell them before you start how high you can jump, if at all, so that they don't suddenly start sailing over gates. Tell them if your pony kicks and whether you can stop him – if you can't, be honest and some-one will put a leading rein in their pocket to be used if necessary. Tell them if your saddle is likely to slip and if your pony can't face double-decker buses.

110

Don't dawdle at the back, or push everyone out of the way and always ride at the front. Try and behave with some sort of manners. And don't fuss, try and enjoy yourself even if you are the worst rider present. After all, someone has to be that.

RIDING WITH SOMEONE ON FOOT OR BICYCLE. Be kind: don't tear up a main road shouting, 'Look, I can ride,' with your mother pedalling furiously behind or, worse still, running, frightened to death that you'll fall off. Have a thought for her and, if you must show off, do it away from traffic. Don't barge into your companion – it's more difficult for him or her to get out of your pony's way, especially on a bicycle. Your father may be tougher, but he is also breakable, so do be careful, and don't expect him to run with you while you gallop, or fly into a rage because he wants to go home after five or six miles. Be grateful that he's bothering with you at all – lots of fathers don't.

RIDING OUT WITH A RIDING SCHOOL. Don't insist on the best pony, other riders may like him too. Don't expect to be in front all the time, or grumble loudly about your mount. Most riding schools give their pupils a quiet animal to start with. Try and be pleasant to the other riders, but don't tell them what to do, that's the instructor's job. Be very helpful. Open and shut gates if you are capable. Pick up fallen riders, or their hats if any are knocked off. Ride as well as you can. If you find the ride dull, you can practise improving your

seat, or making your pony go a bit better, or simply concentrate on changing your diagonals, or riding in one hand. But if the ride is boring because your pony is very young, or very old, or grossly underfed, don't go to that particular riding school again – because the sooner it is closed down the better.

SCHOOLING. If you school your pony with other people it can be fun and very rewarding, and schooling with other people is probably more enjoyable than schooling alone – that is, if you like them. Take it in turns to give the orders. 'Walk on', 'trot on', 'change the rein', and so on. Try and make it fun, even when you're shrieking, 'Heels down, John', or 'Elbows in, Susan'. You can imitate the voices of people you hate, or dress up and pretend to be an irate colonel. But do try not to end with a slanging match, even if you are sure you keep your hands still and Susan says you don't. You will never improve your riding if you can't instruct without quarrelling, and just shriek at each other things like, 'Wrong leg', or 'You're cutting all the corners'. Don't expect instant results. Improving a pony takes time, especially if you are improving yourself as well.

Practise backing between poles on the ground to see if you can back straight. Halt straight at a certain spot, which is much more difficult than it sounds, and never, never lose your temper and start jerking your pony in the mouth, because if you do, he will hate being schooled and then neither of you will enjoy it. Try and choose things to do which are possible for your pony and then go to a rally and see what your instructor says about you. Listen carefully and try to put what he says into practice next time you are schooling.

DRIVING. Driving a pony can be a great way of travelling, but do remember that harness, like tack, has to be cleaned, and there's a lot more of it! It must fit, and you can't harness a pony to a trap without help the first time, because everything must be adjusted properly – collars need to fit, breeching must press on the right part of your pony while going downhill, and traces must be the right length. You will also need somewhere to keep your vehicle snug and dry, or you will soon have grass growing through the floor!

Your pony will need to be trained to go in harness. Don't think you can do this yourself. Find someone who knows about it, even if it means paying. Listen to what he says and

ask him to give you some lessons as well, because driving is an art in itself.

The nicest ponies to drive are strong, brisk ones who are proud of their strength. Lazy ones always look exhausted and after a time you become sorry for them and start walking up even the smallest hill!

Driving gets you about and you don't need to pass a test to do it, or buy petrol. But try to keep to lanes and by-ways, because having a queue of fifty cars behind you, plus a few buses and lorries, is likely to upset the best pony and can be nerve-racking for you.

KEEPING BRIDLE PATHS OPEN. This will, of course, help to make your rides more enjoyable; because, let's face it, being scratched to pieces by brambles, dragged to the ground by branches, or torn to shreds by barbed wire is painful.

If you find a bridle path even partially blocked, do something about it, don't just grumble. Approach your parish council (every parish has one and the vicar can tell you whom to contact), or get in touch with your Pony Club, or the British Horse Society. If rubbish has been dumped, have a look and dig around. You may find some incriminating evidence, an old bill, an envelope with an address on it, which can lead you to the culprit. It's an offence to dump rubbish, as well as a horrible habit, so be a detective and see if you can catch whoever is guilty.

You may find that your parish council or some local society keep paths cleared by their own efforts. If so, why not go and help? You will meet all sorts of people – children, odd characters in deerstalkers, ancient ladies in faded felt hats plus dogs, of course. Take a hedge-cutting tool, or simply help to drag branches to a bonfire. It's a great way of making friends and you will appreciate all the hard work next time you ride along that particular stretch of bridleway.

TAKING YOUR PONY INTO THE HOUSE. This isn't usually feasible, even with the best of parents, but ponies do love seeing *your* stable. Much depends on the floor, of course. Hoofs soon destroy expensive parquet, super new linoleum or vinyl, and disastrous things can happen to carpets. But if your floors are of stone or old-fashioned brick you are reasonably safe from frightful damage being done. I and one of my sisters were once photographed for a magazine, standing on each side of a pony looking out of the front door. We had a yearling called Shandy who came into the kitchen for elevenses. One night, after a rather good dinner, my father left the back door ajar. In the morning the kitchen was in chaos. It has been a wet night and the floor was smeared all over with small, unshod hoofprints; eggs were scattered, the tea caddy upset, the bread bin empty. Shandy, however, was back in his paddock pretending that nothing had happened. So you see, there are dangers!

There must also be room for a pony to turn round, and tiny kitchens are not suitable for visiting sixteen-hand hunters, however agreeable, for once in they may be impossible to get out.

Having Fun without a Pony or Much Money

Join the Pony Club if you can afford the subscription. Go to dismounted rallies and the annual party, and help at mounted rallies. Borrow books from the library and try to be a member of the quiz team.

Go hunting on foot or on a bicycle. Open gates for the hunt staff, take down fences for the field (and put them up again, of course), and catch loose horses. Hunting on foot can be tremendous fun, but don't get in front of the hunt and head the fox. Stay with foot followers who know something – at least to start with.

If you have a local riding school, save up for the odd ride there and then offer to help – but I mean help! No one wants a person getting in everyone's way, smoking, or leaving sweet papers all over the stable yard. Never stand and watch other people work. Offer to groom the other side of a pony, to empty a full wheelbarrow, to clean up the midden, tidy the saddle room, help with the tack, or fill up water buckets. There's always something which needs doing in a stable yard. Don't expect to be given rides in exchange, not straight away, anyway; just help for the joy of it. Get there early if you can, and take your lunch, but ask for permission first. Some of the best riders have started hard up and horseless, so don't despair. People who begin the hard way often end up the best.

You can also offer to help at local shows. Jump stewards are often needed to put up knocked-down poles, or an extra hand may be needed at the gate, or to give out numbers in the secretary's tent.

The saying 'where there's a will, there's a way' can be very true when it comes to riding. So keep on trying and, once you can ride and if you are brave and willing to risk your neck, you may find a mass of mounts at your disposal – four-year-olds which need backing, dealers' ponies which need schooling before they are sold, show ponies which need showing. Or simply a pony down the road which gets laminitis if he isn't exercised regularly. And the more ponies you ride, the better you will be in the end. As you get older, paying jobs may even come your way – trekking stables often need helpers in the summer, polo stables need grooms, saddlery shops need Saturday morning assistants – the possibilities are endless.

Getting to Know Your Pony Better

When he puts his ears flat back you know he's cross – but try to work out why. He may hate another pony, or be tired and want to be left alone. He may be eating, and most ponies hate being patted when they are tucking into a large feed, and I must say I understand their point of view. I wouldn't want my nose stroked, my neck patted, or my hair smoothed, just when I was tucking into the most delicious ice-cream. Would you?

Kicking may be an act of bad temper, or his girths may be pinching or he may just be heartily sick of you pulling his tail or washing his hind legs in ice-cold water. Or he may have a cut, or mud fever.

Looking after a good-tempered pony is much more fun than looking after a vicious one. Most well-managed ones are good-tempered, though, like people, their temperaments vary. We have bought kickers and biters who have never kicked or bitten after their first week with us. Why did they kick before? We don't know. Knowing your pony and seeing what he likes is a way of life, and you win every time because a happy pony will be kind and pleasant, whereas a really angry pony can come back and kick you when you're lying on the ground, stamp on your feet on purpose and bite you at every opportunity.

If your pony likes you, he will often whinny at your approach, he will nuzzle you with his nose, lick you, give your sleeve an affectionate pull. He will rub his head against you, which is what he does to his horsy friends out in the field. Horses are not violent by nature. If yours is, there's something wrong somewhere. Perhaps you are violent with him, or bad-tempered? Perhaps his stable lacks bedding or his field has nothing but earth and ragwort in it, or boys have been throwing stones at him. Perhaps you never appreciate him, however hard he tries (horses thrive on praise). Or perhaps you spoil him, give in to him on every occasion until he has become a bully and only rideable if bribed. If so, he needs firmness and quick retaliation when he bites or kicks. Human bullies are usually unhappy, and it's the same with ponies. He should like you, and you him. This way, you have a companion and friend as well as a pony. You can tell him your troubles and he won't laugh at you, cry into his mane and he will try to cheer you up. He'll always be there for you, perhaps waiting at the gate watching for you coming home from school, and when you call him, he'll gallop across to you like a long-lost friend – perhaps your best friend.

Finally, how much you enjoy your pony is largely up to you. Feed him properly, encourage him, rest him when necessary, and he will enjoy life, too. He will carry you for years; hunting cheerfully all day, winning rosettes, taking you to victory through every sort of trouble. To my mind this is possibly the greatest part of riding, the great combination of horse and rider, be it a riding school pony, show pony, hunter or champion. It is a companionship which nothing else can equal.

Appendix

Some Famous Annual Horse Shows

Attend any of these and you will learn a lot.

Hickstead, Sussex. Easter meeting: usually the first week in April.
Oxford County Show. Last week in April.
Newark and Notts. Show. May.
Royal Windsor Horse Show. May.
Shropshire and West Midland Show. May.
Devon County Show. May.
Suffolk County Show. End of May, beginning of June.
Bath and West Show. End of May, beginning of June.
Royal Highland Show. June.
South of England Show. June.
Royal Norfolk Show. June.
Royal Show. July, often at Kenilworth, Warwickshire.
Great Yorkshire Show. July.
Hickstead. July.
Royal International Horse Show. July.
Greater London Show, Clapham Common. August Bank Holiday
Monday.
Royal Lancashire Show. August.
Hickstead. August, and again in September.
Horse of the Year Show, Wembley. October.

For exact dates and locations consult *Horse and Hound*, or
horsy friends, or your local travel agent.

Horse Trials

Most Pony Clubs run coaches to the larger horse trials. There are about 60 or more every year. For dates and locations, look for posters in local saddlers' shops, in your local paper and in *Horse and Hound*. The five below are three-day horse trials of international repute.

Badminton, Gloucestershire. April.
Tidworth, Wiltshire. May.
Bramham Park, Yorkshire. June.
Burghley, Lincolnshire. September.
Wylye, Wiltshire. October.

The Pony Club Horse Trial Championships take place at Stoneleigh, in Warwickshire, at the end of August.

Some Polo Grounds

Smith's Lawn, Windsor, or Windsor Great Park.
Cirencester, Gloucestershire.
Cowdray Park, Sussex.
Oulton Park, Cheshire.
Ham House, Richmond, Surrey.
Rhine Field, Brockenhurst, Hampshire.
Stourhead, near Mere, Wiltshire.

If you want to find out more about adult polo, try Brig. J. R. C. Cannon, C.B.E., M.V.O., Hurlingham Polo Association, Mark Lane, London EC3R.

Some Information for Would-be Pony Trekkers

Buy: *A Guide To Pony Trekking and Mounted Expeditions*, a Pony Club publication from The National Equestrian Centre, Kenilworth, Warwickshire, CV8 2LR.

For a list of approved centres, write to: The Ponies of Britain Club, Brookside Farm, Ascot, Berks.

For details of the 80-mile bridleway from Eastbourne in Sussex to Petersfield in Hampshire, write to: The National Parks Commission, 1 Cambridge Gate, London N.W.1. Details of accommodation for this route and grazing can be had from: The Association of Sussex Downsmen, 93 Church Street, Hove, Sussex.

For the Yorkshire Moors and Coast route, write to: The County Hall, York. For the Yorkshire Dales, write to: The West Riding County Planning Office, 71 Northgate, Wakefield, Yorkshire.

For treks in Wales, consult: The Secretary, Pony Trekking Centre of Wales, P.O. Box 1, Builth Wells, Breconshire.

For Scotland, consult: The Scottish Tourist Board, Rutland Place, Edinburgh.

For details of Youth Hostels which can provide you with a dry bed and a hot meal, write to: The Y.H.A., Trevelyan House, St. Albans, Herts, enclosing a stamped, self-addressed envelope.

For pony trekking abroad consult your local travel agent.

For musical rides with diagrams, buy *Mounted Games And Gymkhanas*, from the British Horse Society, National Equestrian Centre, Kenilworth, Warwickshire, CV8 2LR.

For information about the Pony Club, its teams, polo, etc., consult your Pony Club secretary, or write to: Pony Club Headquarters, National Equestrian Centre, Kenilworth, Warwickshire, CV8 2LR.

125

For help with driving, write to: The Secretary, The British Driving Society, 10 Marley Avenue, New Milton, Hampshire.

For registering your pony, try: National Pony Society, Stoke Lodge, 85 Cliddesden Road, Basingstoke, Hampshire.

For reporting cruelty to horses, try your local telephone directory for the R.S.P.C.A., or write to: The Royal Society for the Prevention of Cruelty to Animals, 105 Jermyn Street, London, S.W.1.

For the address of your nearest branch of the R.D.A., write to: Riding for the Disabled Association, Avenue R, National Agricultural Centre, Kenilworth, Warwickshire CV8 2LY.

For details of show jumping and for registering youself and/or your pony for jumping, write to: The B.S.J.A., The National Equestrian Centre, Kenilworth, Warwickshire, CV8 2LR.

If you can't find a registered riding school near your home, write to: The Association of British Riding Schools, Chesham House, 56 Green End Road, Sawtry, Huntingdon, PE17 5OY.

Show Jumping Rules (Abbreviated)

Riding dress should be worn
A whip longer than 30 inches may not be carried
Knock-down by fore or hind legs – four faults
1st refusal, stop or run out – three faults
2nd refusal, stop or run out – six faults
3rd refusal on course – elimination
Turning a circle, or your pony's quarters towards a jump constitutes a refusal
Fall of horse and rider – eight faults
Fall of rider – eight faults
Starting before bell, failing to ride through start or finishing line, leaving the ring before completing course – elimination

Breaking rules – elimination
Riding lame, sick or exhausted horse – elimination
Cruelty in ring – elimination
There can be a time limit. If you exceed it, you face elimination.
   There is rarely a time limit, however, at small shows.

For a more complete set of rules, apply to: B.S.J.A., National
Equestrian Centre, Stoneleigh, Kenilworth, Warwickshire, enclosing 25p.

For Prince Philip Cup rules and for Tetrathlon rules, write to:
The Pony Club Headquarters, National Equestrian Centre,
Kenilworth, Warwickshire, for leaflets, price 5p each.

Horse Trial Penalties (Abbreviated)

First refusal, run out or circle at fence – 10 penalty points
Second run out, circle or refusal at same fence – 20 penalty points
Third run out, circle or refusal at same obstacle – elimination
Fall of horse and/or rider at obstacle – 30 penalty points
(The above points are cumulative)
Error on course not put right – elimination
Horse resisting for sixty consecutive seconds anywhere on the
   course – elimination
Every commenced period of five seconds in excess of time
   allowed – 1 penalty point
Exceeding the time limit – elimination
Continuing the course without a hat – elimination

For more detailed rules and a general description of obstacles,
etc., at the Pony Club Horse Trials, write for leaflet from the
Pony Club Headquarters, National Equestrian Centre, Kenilworth, Warwickshire, price 5p.